LEADING
MADE EASY

Praise for **Leading Made Easy**

"Appreciate the common sense approach to leadership that isn't always common practice. **Leading Made Easy** reminds leaders of the behaviors necessary to effectively lead and develop people. The author delivers it in such a way that leaders cannot only relate, but also immediately understand how to apply it to their own journey. As leaders, we can never be reminded enough of what it takes to lead successfully. This book does just that!"

— Hope Zoeller, Ed.D.,
Founder & President, HOPE (Helping Other People Excel), LLC
Author of *HOPE For Leaders Unabridged*

"If you are a seasoned leader, **Leading Made Easy** will refresh you. If you are a new leader, you will be inspired by it! Dr. Johnson uses the **LEAD** acronym to present four leadership principles that will enhance leadership effectiveness for anyone, at any level of the organization. The behaviors that he outlines for each principle are easy to understand and apply to real world situations. This book is an excellent resource for any leader wishing to improve his or her effectiveness!"

— Davis M. Robinson, PhD,
CEO & President of Horizon Consulting Services, LLC
Author of *Discipline Your Motivation*

"Wow! A book on leadership that is an easy read—a first for me! In **Leading Made Easy**, you'll find yourself immersed in many interesting leadership stories, and before you know it, you will have gained new knowledge that is easy to apply in your leadership role. This book provides common sense tips and insights about leadership behaviors, which many of us have forgotten in this era of technology. This is a must read for everyone who wants to positively influence self-growth and the performance of his or her organization, team, or family!"

— Miriam Wallace,
Vice President, Human Resources, JourneyCare, Inc.

"Alonzo makes the subject of leadership relevant and with at-your-fingertips ease. LEAD is an acronym that punches four valuable principles. These principles are derived from his exceptional career journey. The principles and behaviors apply to life, as well as work-life. Everyone can learn from Alonzo's style—he reads like cool jazz, lyrically flowing through his messages with perfectly toned scenarios. Pow!"

— Marigrace McKay
OCMAdvantage Consulting, Organization and People Solutions
Contributing Author, *Lessons in Leadership*

LEADING
MADE EASY

Four Principles for Leadership Effectiveness

Alonzo Johnson, Ph.D.

FOREWORD BY
Joel D. Weeks

OASYS Press ◊ McDonough, GA

Leading Made Easy:
Four Principles for Leadership Effectiveness

Printed in the United States of America
First Edition, 2016

22 21 20 19 18 17 16 1 2 3 4 5

978-0-9863965-3-3 (paperback)
978-0-9863965-4-0 (e-book)

Visit the author's websites:
www.AlonzoJohnsonPHD.com
www.Leading-Made-Easy.com
www.LEAD360Assessment.com

Cover and book design by Kevin Williamson

◊◊◊◊◊

Leading Made Easy is available for sale at special quantity discounts. For more information, please visit AlonzoJohnsonPHD.com or Leading-Made-Easy.com or email inquiries to info@AlonzoJohnsonPHD.com.

THE MADE EASY SERIES

This book is dedicated to the memories of my
mother, Amanda Cobbs-Johnson;
father, Girther Johnson; and
grandmother, Francis Kennedy-Harper—

Who sacrificed greatly so that I may thrive.

Incepto ne desistam.

— A.J. —

ACKNOWLEDGEMENT

Isaac Newton once said, "If I have seen further than others, it is by standing upon the shoulders of giants." I am grateful to the giants in my life who have allowed me to stand upon their shoulders to see possibilities. You have inspired me to explore the meaning of effective leadership and supported me throughout this book-writing process.

To Annmarie Buchanan, who was my sounding board and mainstay throughout this project—thank you!

I would like to acknowledge Jeff Corkran, Joe DeSensi, Tom Norris, and Frances Paschall for helping with editing and organizing this book, and many others who took the time to read the manuscript and provide valuable feedback.

A big thank you to Dr. Joseph Petrosko for helping with the statistical validation of the behaviors and attributes for the LEAD principles presented in this book.

I would also like to thank all the individuals who have trusted me to lead and mentor them, and the numerous participants who attended my leadership development workshops—I learned so much about leadership from you.

I am especially grateful to Dr. Carolyn R. Parkins, Mike Goldberg, and other leaders who have pointed the way for me through coaching and mentoring over the years—thank you for allowing me to stand upon your shoulders.

I'm eternally grateful!

Contents

FOREWORD

When I first met Alonzo Johnson many years ago in the military, he was already a star performer. Having been placed in a leadership role higher than the one to which soldiers of his rank are normally assigned, he was executing the duties and functions of that role better than most officers who were normally assigned to such positions. It was my privilege to watch him over the span of a few years developing, implementing, refining, and exemplifying a great many of the precepts he examines in these pages. In the intervening years, he has continued his tradition of leadership excellence, while holding senior positions within the military, academia, corporate America, and as a business owner.

In four short chapters, Dr. Johnson has distilled the essence of leadership into definable, observable, teachable, and learnable behaviors anyone can put into practice immediately. Properly understood and executed, these attributes will serve to better individuals not only now, in their current roles, but even more importantly, prepare them for greater service to themselves, their organizations, and others with whom they work.

The four leadership principles from which Dr. Johnson has cleverly created the acronym LEAD—**L**earn from Mistakes, **E**xemplify Competence, **A**dd Value, and **D**o the Right Thing—are presented in such a way as to resonate with anyone who has ever been in the workforce at any level. It doesn't matter where readers of this excellent primer are with respect to their position within an organization. *Everyone* can benefit from this common-sense, fresh approach to a topic that has been written about since organizations were first created.

The layout of the book follows the acronym, and Dr. Johnson explores each component of the acronym by providing five separate behaviors that buttress each one. The book draws from dozens of real-life examples from the spectrum of life's activities, each one convincingly supporting the assertions Dr. Johnson makes.

Don't let the small size of the book fool you. It is overflowing with practical prescriptive advice on a multitude of tasks and subtasks confronting today's leaders, including those salient workplace topics many leaders shy away from—how to counsel team members, how to motivate underperforming associates, how to regularly conduct a self-evaluation, and how to make critical decisions in a timely manner. His treatment of these issues alone makes this book a worthwhile addition to any leader's reading list.

Any number of different leadership approaches can be taken when directing and inspiring a group of individuals to accomplish an objective. Similarly, whoever reads this book can use it in any number of ways to improve his or her leadership competence. You can read the entire book in a short sitting, or just focus on skill areas needing strengthening. You can even learn strategies to solidify the followership of your team members. As the old Disney® commercial used to say, "the possibilities are endless." Let this book help you achieve your leadership possibilities!

— Joel D. Weeks
Colonel, U.S. Army (retired)

INTRODUCTION

According to Warren Bennis, "Becoming a leader is synonymous with becoming yourself. It is precisely that simple, and it is also that difficult."

We tend to over-complicate things in life—and improving one's leadership effectiveness is no exception. With the vast number of leadership theories, models, and principles available, there are myriads of approaches that leaders can use to guide their growth.

When choosing a path to leadership effectiveness, leaders should consider the difference between successful leaders and effective leaders. There are a number of leaders who are successful, in terms of compensation and status; however, successful leaders are not always effective.

Most leaders want to be effective by inspiring and motivating their teams beyond what they thought possible. But finding the approach that works best for them as individuals can be daunting. Receiving guidance of some sort to help sift through the maze of leadership development options tends to help.

For me, that initial guidance came while I was in the military serving in Bamberg, Germany. Each Wednesday afternoon, without fail, my commander would gather his platoon leaders together for a discussion about leadership. He used case studies to help generate and guide the discussions. Each week, he assigned us a new case study to read in order to prepare us for the next week's session.

After each session, he encouraged us to go out and practice the concepts we'd discussed. Having the ability to explore leadership concepts and theories through case studies and discussions, and then actually practice using them, was like working with my father to put together a new bike and then learning to ride it.

I eagerly participated in the weekly leadership discussions and then practiced what I had learned with my team. The leadership lessons that we gleaned and practiced as a result of these discussions became evident to others, especially when we deployed for training exercises. We became known as the best maneuver unit in the entire regiment.

Since that time, I have completed numerous leadership development programs and courses *and* read many books on the subject. In fact, the focus of my doctoral studies was on organizational leadership. All of these experiences have been beneficial; but for me, the leadership discussions that my troop commander facilitated remain the most meaningful leadership development experience.

I believe the guidance that I received during those discussions focused my attention on specific leadership behaviors that were relevant to my needs. In other words, he helped make learning to lead easy.

WHY THIS BOOK?

Leading Made Easy is my effort to channel the leadership discussions that were instrumental in shaping my formative years as a leader, as well as the body of work in leadership that I have amassed through sundry means over the years. The goal is to model the case study format to engage leaders on critical leadership behaviors so that they can internalize and practice them and become more effective, regardless of the environment in which they must operate.

Focusing on these behaviors will not only make learning to lead easier but will also make the *act* of leading easy. *Leading Made Easy* is based on the acronym LEAD, which espouses four research-based principles that many leaders (including myself) have relied on over the years to lead effectively in different environments:

- ☑ **LEARN FROM MISTAKES**
- ☑ **EXEMPLIFY COMPETENCE**
- ☑ **ADD VALUE**
- ☑ **DO THE RIGHT THING**

Furthermore, I have identified **five statistically valid behaviors underpinning each of these four principles.** My hope is that these 20 behaviors will provide focus for those wishing to hone their leadership effectiveness skills.

WHO SHOULD READ THIS BOOK?

Leading Made Easy is the second book in the *Made Easy* series. The first book, *Hiring Made Easy as PIE*, is written primarily for hiring managers with little hiring experience. Accordingly, it presents a straightforward approach for interviewing and selecting best-fit employees.

This book explores how to lead effectively after the hiring process is over, and is intended for anyone desiring to improve his or her leadership effectiveness. Although the principles presented in this book can be scaled and used at any leadership level, this book is written in an easy-to-read format and with easy-to-understand terms and leadership concepts.

HOW TO USE THIS BOOK

Leading Made Easy presents four leadership principles and associated behaviors for leadership effectiveness. There are three options for navigating this book:

1. Read it from cover to cover.
2. Read only the principle in which you think you need the most improvement.
3. Review any part of it as a reference.

An end-of-section reflection activity is included for each principle. The activity provides an opportunity for you to informally assess the degree to which you use the related behaviors presented in this book.

For a more comprehensive evaluation, a companion 360° leadership assessment instrument (*LEAD 360*) is available with this book. The instrument provides the results of a leader's effectiveness from multiple raters (self, boss, direct reports, peers, and others) who have assessed the degree to which the leader practices the principles and associated behaviors. For more information on how to take advantage of the *LEAD 360*, visit **www.AlonzoJohnsonPHD.com** or **www.lead360assessment.com.**

PRINCIPLE ONE
LEARN FROM MISTAKES

I recall my days as a preschooler. I loved to play by jumping from the top of furniture (bed, sofa, chairs, etc.). And what child doesn't? I didn't quite understand my parents' words of caution that I could hurt myself by playing this way. So, I usually didn't listen to their instructions to *stop jumping off the furniture.* After asking me several times to stop, to no avail, my grandmother would say, "Bought sense is better than any." How was I to understand what she meant by that statement? This was just something that grown-ups said.

As fate would have it, I took a nasty fall one day shortly after being asked not to jump from the furniture. While I didn't sustain any major injuries, the fall resulted in a couple of painfully skinned knees, and it taught me to seek alternative play activities to amuse myself.

Although I had been constantly asked to stop jumping from the furniture, it took the mistake of falling and sustaining injuries before I learned to heed my parents' advice. (I had bought sense by paying with skinned knees.)

I have since learned from many mistakes that I have made throughout life—both personally and professionally.

Some of these mistakes were consequential. For example, early on in my military career, I learned about the importance of proper communication by making a mistake that caused a lot of military firepower to be diverted unnecessarily to stave off a threat that did not exist.

Yes, you read that right. Because I did not communicate effectively about the sighting of a possible enemy threat, I came very close to causing conflict between armies of the (then-) Soviet Union and the United States! Here is what happened:

A few years into my military career, I found myself in Germany on a three-year tour as a leader of a platoon within an Armored Cavalry Troop.

In addition to training my platoon to be ready to fight and win against communist aggression, I was responsible for leading surveillance missions along the East/West German Border—the Iron Curtain, as it was then called.

One morning, I decided to take my platoon away from the border camp for practice drills near the border. The area that I chose for these drills was called the "Ghost Autobahn." It consisted of rolling terrain with wooded patches of land and an abandoned highway running through it. The highway had been built in the 1930s as part of the expansive *autobahn* project during the reign of Adolf Hitler.

As we practiced the drills, my lead scout reported that he was observing a possible Soviet tank on the West (friendly) side of the border. Seeing a Soviet tank in our border sector was very unusual, let alone on the friendly side of the border. If the sighting could be confirmed, it might have meant the beginning of a Soviet invasion.

The lead scout's report of the possible sighting prompted me to take the following actions:

1. Order the commanders of the scout vehicles and tanks to move into an observation position to observe and monitor any activity from the possible Soviet tank.
2. Order the lead scout to move his vehicle closer to confirm it was indeed a Soviet tank.

3. Notify the Operation Center that we'd spotted a possible Soviet tank on the West side of the border. I informed them that the lead scout was moving in for a closer look to confirm the sighting, and that I would report back as soon as we could conclusively identify the vehicle.

As the lead scout maneuvered closer to the location of the sighting, I began hearing an increasing level of chatter over the radio. It was communication among the remaining forces at the border camp. They were preparing to deploy to the border and join my platoon to help stave off a Soviet invasion.

The Operation Center did not wait for my confirmation of the possible Soviet tank sighting. Instead, they put the entire border camp on alert and informed the next level of leadership—who put the Attack Helicopter Squadron on alert.

My reporting of a possible Soviet tank sighting created the cascading effect of alerting and readying a large volume of combat forces to engage the enemy.

Once the lead scout reached a distance where he could conclusively identify the sighted object, he radioed to inform me that it was a *hay bailer* that we had observed from a distance, and not a Soviet main battle tank. I promptly informed the Operations Center of the findings.

Of course, my Troop Commander was none too pleased with me and personally ordered me back to the camp with my platoon.

This incident, without a doubt, ranked among the most embarrassing moments of my life.

The important lesson I learned from this mistake was that *effective communication is a two-way process*—not one-way. I realized later that I should have asked the radio operator at the Operations Center to repeat my report back to me, so that I could confirm that he completely understood what I'd said to him.

The lesson from this mistake has stayed with me since that unfortunate event. Nowadays I ask questions or ask the person to whom I'm giving instructions to restate what I said to confirm that the message was understood.

Leaders who learn from their mistakes are able to use their new learning to succeed quicker than those who do not. A leader who learns from mistakes seems to have the ability to leverage the following behaviors:

- ☐ **BEING OPEN TO NEW IDEAS**
- ☐ **LEARNS ON THE FLY**
- ☐ **TAKES RISKS**
- ☐ **REFLECTS ON EXPERIENCES**
- ☐ **ACCEPTS MISTAKES AS OPPORTUNITIES**

BEING OPEN TO NEW IDEAS

Innovative and highly receptive of different approaches to completing tasks

---

One trap into which many leaders fall is the belief that they have the best ideas and ways forward. Others fall victim to their own need to appear strong and determined, even when they don't know the best course. Some of the more hard-headed among them confuse stubbornness with strength. Other times, a leader simply may not know how to ask for input or help.

To be effective, leaders have to be able to open themselves to new ways of thinking and must **constantly look for better ways to do things**. Whether learning a routine skill, or mastering a required task or job that is beyond their current skill set (stretch assignment), leaders must be willing to **use**

innovative approaches to solve problems, especially when new thinking or ways of doing things could drastically enhance outcomes.

History is fraught with leaders whose *openness to new ideas* has changed the status quo and created life-changing innovations that are critical to modern-day life. Wilbur and Orville Wright are examples of such leaders. These aviation pioneers are credited with achieving the first powered, sustained, and controlled heavier-than-air flight in 1903. Two years later, they built and flew the first two-passenger airplane, which has evolved into what is known as a jetliner today, and a common way of travel.

Steve Jobs is another leader who **demonstrated the capacity to innovate.** His openness to new ideas gave the world the iPod, iPhone, and iPad, and ushered in a new era of miniature smart devices using touch-sensitive technologies. A 2015 survey conducted by the Pew Research Center found that 68% of Americans owned smartphones and 45% of them owned tablet computers. The ownership of these devices is likely to increase as people around the world become more dependent upon this technology.

As we see in these examples, effective leaders are willing to try new approaches to solving old problems. They are curious and **question the status quo in order to uncover new methods for doing things.** They never seem satisfied with their current skills and knowledge and are continuously seeking to improve them to enhance their leadership skills.

Remaining open to new ideas allows leaders to **generate new ideas by examining issues from different perspectives.** This, in turn, places a few requirements upon the leaders. They must first make it possible for new ideas to be voiced; they have to invite people to give their ideas and constructive feedback, and do so in a way that doesn't penalize unorthodox thinking (or blunt honesty). Then, once people have had a chance to give leaders their thoughts, the second challenge is remaining intellectually open to the new ideas in those thoughts. If you're a leader, you must ask yourself: *What am I not seeing? What lines of thought have I not completely entertained?*

Remaining open to new ideas is challenging because we have to be willing to separate ideas from the context of the person providing them and remain objective. This means that our own ideas, which we all naturally prefer, can no longer rank higher than anyone else's. It doesn't matter if you don't like or trust someone; it doesn't matter if they rank below you; it doesn't matter if they've been wrong every time before. As someone once said, even a broken clock is right twice a day—and all readings have to be given their merit. You never know who will be right, or who will provide the "missing piece" to a new and successful idea.

When leaders open themselves to new ideas from members of their team, they often find a bottomless gold mine of ideas. Sure, not every suggestion will have merit, but that's what miners do; they work through the dirt and rocks to find the morsels of substance, then others process and combine them to make beautiful things.

Mistakes and failure are a natural part of the process of being open to new ideas. The Wright brothers and Steve Jobs failed many times before they succeeded—as did many other successful, yet effective leaders throughout history. Michael Jordan, who is among the most accomplished basketball players of all times, earned that distinction due to his ability to learn from his mistakes. He once said, "I've missed more than 9,000 shots in my career. I've lost almost 300 games. Twenty-six times I've been trusted to take the game-winning shot and missed. I've failed over and over and over again in my life. And that is why I succeed."

Remaining open to new ideas will position you to grow and succeed as well!

In summary, a leader who is open to new ideas . . .

- Uses innovative approaches to solve problems
- Is constantly looking for better ways to do things
- Demonstrates the capacity to innovate
- Generates new ideas by examining issues from different perspectives
- Questions the status quo to uncover new methods for doing things

---

LEARNS ON THE FLY

Quickly grasps new concepts, strategies, and skills necessary to function effectively in a new environment.

Another behavior exhibited by leaders who learn from their mistakes is the ability to *learn on the fly*, or quickly adapt the right skills and strategies in a new situation. *Learning on the fly* really refers to a specific set of attributes, any of which can be displayed in tandem by the leader. These attributes are:

- **Using a variety of strategies to learn on the job**
- **Quickly developing an understanding of complex situations**
- **Rapidly discovering new approaches to doing things**
- **Generating a variety of options to find solutions**
- **Quickly mastering skills and knowledge required to perform new tasks**

Let's examine the *learning on the fly* behavior through the lens of someone who is in a leadership role at a restaurant. You probably have a favorite restaurant that you frequent or would like to patronize more. Restaurant work is challenging because it requires that many different employees all work closely together—not just to cook the food correctly and deliver it quickly but to preserve the perfect experience for guests. This symphony requires teamwork from managers, bartenders, chefs, cooks, servers, dishwashers, hostesses, and sometimes other players, too.

You can't say some jobs are more important than others; a competent dishwasher is just as important as a world-class chef because if you can't get a clean plate, the quality of the food won't matter.

Since every job is important in a functioning, high-performance team, and everyone on that team is required to understand a complex situation in similar ways, the restaurant leader must be able to quickly develop a good grasp of everyone's roles so that he or she can continuously improve the team's performance. The leader who learns on the fly should also challenge team members to learn each other's roles. In doing so, team members can enhance their skills and strengthen their performance to become a more agile team. After all, a team with a high level of skills is an asset for effective leadership.

The restaurant example is one with which most people will be able to easily identify. What about an extraordinary example? Consider the story of Erin Brockovich (depicted in a film of the same name starring Julia Roberts). Erin was a single mother of three, who lost her job and struggled to find another. Making matters worse, she was hit by another driver, causing a neck injury, and her attorney Ed Masry was unable to earn a settlement for her. Desperate, she visited his California law office looking for a job and managed to land one working as his paralegal, even though she had no background in law or even a college degree.

While working in Ed's office, Erin discovered a curious pattern. During a meeting with a client about her real estate deal with Pacific Gas and Electric (PG&E), she noticed medical records in the same file. The client, Donna Jensen, explained that she kept all PG&E correspondence in one file, and that PG&E had helped her family cover certain medical bills related to their illnesses. Erin asked Donna why they'd done that; Donna explained that it was "because of the chromium," *chromium* being a groundwater byproduct of the power plant's activity in the city of Hinkley, California. PG&E informed the residents of Hinkley that it was a safe form of chromium when in reality it was carcinogenic and was causing serious illnesses—everything from cancer and leukemia to immune deficiencies and asthma.

Erin wound up spearheading a massive class-action lawsuit against PG&E which, in the end, paid more than $300 million in damages to the residents of Hinkley. Aside from her heart and passion, what made it possible for Erin to accomplish so much—despite having no formal background in law—was her formidable ability to learn on the fly.

Despite being (humorously) headstrong and potty-mouthed, Erin proved herself a good listener and a patient learner, equally willing to read for hours on end or consult with Ed, as well as professionals in different fields. She was able to grasp the complexity of the situation between Hinkley and PG&E, including all of the smaller players like litigators, doctors, and researchers because she was willing to learn something about each person involved. She was willing to discover new approaches to the overarching problem. Whenever she hit one dead end with research, she turned around and tried the next route forward. Erin mastered the basics quickly and didn't hesitate to dive straight into the harder work.

Though most work lacks the second-to-second rush of a restaurant, or the moral immediacy of Erin Brockovich's lawsuits, most work does follow the basic pattern of these examples: a business opens its doors to serve people with a particular need, and people get jobs serving a particular role for that business. In turn, the people who work for that business cannot work in isolation; they have to be able to learn in changing circumstances and not just at their own pace. Effective leaders especially must quickly learn the strengths of their team members and identify those who are able to rise to these changing circumstances and learn on the fly. Those who can learn more and apply it more quickly, by default or by choice, are those who have the greatest potential for growth and leadership.

In summary, a leader who learns on the fly . . .

- Uses a variety of strategies to learn on the job
- Quickly develops an understanding of complex situations
- Rapidly discovers new approaches to doing things
- Generates a variety of options to find solutions
- Quickly masters skills and knowledge required to perform new tasks

---

TAKING RISKS

Takes on unfamiliar tasks and stretch assignments when success is not assured

---

A third leadership behavior for learning from mistakes is *taking risks*. While we often think of risk as "danger," something to be avoided, the truth is that danger and opportunity often look quite a bit alike—and the greatest potential in people, teams, and even the development of humankind often rests in ideas that seem dangerous when they're born.

Consider, for example, Copernicus and his theory of *heliocentricity*: the notion that the sun, not Earth, was the center of our solar system. While heliocentricity has since been proven correct (we have photographic evidence now), it was once a "dangerous idea"; the notion that Earth and human beings were *not* at the center of creation was quite upsetting to many, and it made Copernicus many powerful enemies. Yet we remember Copernicus's name because he took the risk of introducing a controversial (but constructive and valid) idea to the world, even before the world might have been "ready."

One aspect of taking risks is a willingness to **use unconventional approaches to achieve goals.** Sometimes, if a conventional approach isn't working, there isn't anything conventional that will make it work; what's required is someone willing to chance that the unusual will provide a solution, or even a breakthrough success.

Here's another risky idea that became a staple of modern-day living: *overnight package delivery*. By now, most people in America can't remember a time when next day delivery wasn't available. But overnight delivery was once a highly unusual practice. Most packages were shipped by trucks or passenger airlines and usually required several days to reach their destinations.

It wasn't until Fred Smith took a risk on an idea that overnight delivery was born. While completing his undergraduate studies at Yale University in the 1960s, Smith wrote a term paper outlining a new approach to package delivery—express delivery. But his professor did not view the concept as revolutionary and gave Smith an average grade for the paper.

In 1973, Smith's vision of express delivery came to fruition, as his new company, Federal Express (FedEx) began launching delivery flights from its operation center in Memphis, Tennessee. FedEx had challenges initially that likely caused Smith to question whether his professor had been right about his express delivery idea.

Shortly after the company started, its funds dwindled to only $5,000—not enough to fuel the planes to continue operating. Smith tried to get a loan and was denied. With his high level of risk tolerance, Smith then flew to Las Vegas and used the remaining money to gamble. He won enough money to continue operating until he eventually secured a loan.

The FedEx example highlights another important attribute of risk-taking: **employing critical thinking skills to help manage risks.** Within a "conventional" mentality, Smith might have sold some of his planes to raise enough money to continue operating, or filed bankruptcy. Instead, he thought critically to determine whether he'd be playing a losing game, or if he'd be better off taking a chance on something that could flip the table and keep the business afloat. He questioned all of his assumptions and those of others. In the end, he decided that risk was his only path to any real reward. Today, FedEx is ranked among companies that earn billions of dollars annually. Does his risk seem so strange now?

Let's consider one final example of risk-taking leadership: Elon Musk. If you haven't heard of him, you might have heard of some of the companies he's founded, among them PayPal, Tesla Motors, Solar City, and SpaceX. Musk competes with other strong minds for the leadership of today's industries, but the quality that sets him apart from the pack is his eye for calculation—and a tolerance for risks on a scale most people can't imagine.

At 27, he sold his first company, Zip2, for personal proceeds of $22 million. Three years later, PayPal sold to eBay and netted him another $165 million. At 30, he could have waltzed off into the sunset with about $180 million, never to worry about anything again. Instead, he invested in not just one, but *three* huge and risky ideas: an electric car startup, a massive solar-energy project, and a company with a goal of the eventual colonization of Mars. No, he wasn't kidding; if anything, he was painfully matter-of-fact.

It'd be one thing if Musk were just a genius or visionary, if he'd used his reputation and his skills to find funding and ultimately lead people to achieve the companies' visions. What seals his place in history is that not only did he do just that, but he also staked every last dollar of his own money to make sure those companies (Tesla, Solar City, and SpaceX, respectively) would have a shot at succeeding. There was a time, he explains, when during all of this development he had to borrow money for rent. If those companies had failed—and each one, independently, was likely to fail—he would have been reduced to nothing, all the way down from hundreds of millions of dollars.

Elon Musk is proof that sometimes success requires risk. Risk was not an optional component of the ventures Musk was undertaking; all of them were, by definition, risky, challenging, and exceedingly difficult. Tesla, for example, was an electric car startup business that would compete with everyone in the automotive market—huge players—and it was founded at a time when consumers weren't that interested in electric cars, especially not expensive ones. But his idea seems to have stuck, and Tesla is now successful beyond what seemed possible when it was founded.

There are two other attributes of risk that effective leaders illustrate. One is that **risk-taking is a necessary component of success**; another is that leaders must often **make responsible decisions despite having incomplete information.** The word decision comes from a Latin root meaning "to cut"—by nature, leaders making decisions must choose a course of action by favoring the most helpful insights and information and "cutting out" the rest.

The last attribute we will discuss for risk-taking leaders is an understanding of its challenge to the spirit: to take a risk is to **welcome the challenges of the unknown.** It's the unknown that contains the greatest potential and holds the future we can't yet see—whether or not we're afraid of the unknown is our choice. If the situation calls for taking a chance, a leader will take it; if there isn't really a choice, why be afraid of it?

In summary, a leader who takes risks . . .

- Often uses unconventional approaches to achieve goals
- Employs critical thinking skills to help manage risks
- Makes responsible decisions despite incomplete or inadequate information
- Demonstrates that risk-taking is a necessary component of being successful
- Welcomes the challenge of the unknown

REFLECTING ON EXPERIENCES

Considers past accomplishments and failures when envisioning future possibilities

Learning from mistakes is a valuable (and necessary) leadership quality for a reason we don't often think about: life is full of repetitive cycles, and most mistakes you make will repeat themselves until you correct yourself. Whether it's how to spell certain words correctly, how to tie your shoelaces, or how to compose yourself for a speech, you'll get it wrong every time until you practice getting it right. The goal for each of us, as we go along, is to make fewer mistakes and get better at the things we do.

Reflection is seminal to being an effective leader—whether it is reflecting on one's own experience or experience gained by others. One of the workplace tools designed specifically for this purpose is an after-action review, or AAR. The military is especially good at AARs, and they're used in many corporate and team-work settings. Despite the official-sounding name, they can be carried out whenever you need—on yourself, your team, or after any type of event. The idea of an AAR, in a nutshell, is this: taking a moment after something has happened to assess what happened. *What could we have done better or worse? What was supposed to happen, and what actually did? What worked and what didn't?*

AARs can be informal, or they can be short and straight to the point—and they often are. After all, if an AAR is done correctly, the people in a given situation will have just experienced what happened; they will have a chance to directly connect theory to reality and turn unconscious learning into tacit and clear information.

To use a slightly more precise word, life is *iterative*—we go through certain loops, improving as we go with tools like the AAR. As we improve we might hope for *mastery*, for the gradual improvements over time to accumulate. As with bakery treats, they're perfect because the conscientious baker has made them thousands of times before, each time improving on the last batch.

We might also hope for *success*, that by completing enough loops we can accomplish something bigger or better; the same baker, aware of his profit margins and wanting a vacation, might calculate that he needs ten more big days (ten "good circuits" of the loop) to pay for it. Without reflecting on what is truly important and working towards that goal, leaders will end up in a constant loop (think "hamster in a cage") getting the same results each time. We're aware of life's iterations, and we all use them to think about the things that we want.

Leaders learn from mistakes and must be especially adept at **reflecting on the past to envision future possibilities.** This ability will give them valuable insights for improving and adapting their skills. In some way, leaders are keenly aware of how the events of the past (successes or failures) can inform the present and future; the best leaders consider every past insight they can. As Margaret J. Wheatley once said, "Without reflection, we go blindly on our way, creating more unintended consequences, and failing to achieve anything useful."

There are four specific attributes of reflective leaders that allow them to be successful:

1. **Leveraging *experience* to make decisions.** Leaders make decisions on the basis of some artifact. Sometimes the artifact is statistics and data; sometimes it's anecdotal or qualitative evidence, and sometimes it's just hearsay, rumor, or a "gut feeling." Each of these can present a compelling reason of its own depending on the situation, but none are as reliable as applicable or relevant experience. If something is happening, or about to happen, it stands to reason that it'd be most

helpful to start with what happened last time, whether the experience is the leader's own or something offered by another team member. All of the other considerations, like available data (not supported by lived experience) and one's own opinion, tend to fall silent (or take on new contextual meaning) in the recollection of an experience both similar and informative to the situation at hand. Leaders guide teams towards these sources of insight whenever and wherever they're available.

2. **Learning from both accomplishments and setbacks.** Our natural temptation as problem-solvers is to focus on what does not work, or what did not go well. If anyone is to succeed in the long run, it's essential to correct mistakes and learn from failures—but we often forget to examine our accomplishments and successes, too, and we can often learn just as much from them.

3. **Wanting to know what went right, what went wrong, and why each of these occurred.** Going one step further, true leaders don't stop at simply knowing their successes and failures, and what to change next time, they also go to lengths to understand the causes of their success and failure. Accordingly, they are analysts and not merely observers of their own history.

4. **Using constructive feedback from others to improve performance.** Being open to others' perceptions, while having the flexibility to change when opportunities present, is paramount to the reflective leader's effectiveness. Follow-through is always important, and this is no less true when reflecting on past experiences. Good reflection and analysis without open discussion or setting conclusive plans for the future is like baking a beautiful cake and then deciding to throw it away before anyone gets to indulge and provide you with culinary reviews—no one benefits.

To that end, strong leaders will invest in good, consistent, and constructive feedback mechanisms throughout their tenure as team leaders or as followers. When team members are doing well they should be praised, and they should be directed and educated in areas needing improvement. This wouldn't all be complete unless the leader followed his or her own advice and made sure to seek out feedback for personal and professional development, both positive and constructive.

In summary, a leader who reflects on experience . . .

- Leverages his or her experience to make decisions
- Learns from both accomplishments and setbacks
- Wants to know what went right and wrong and why each of these occurred
- Reflects on the past to envision future possibilities
- Uses constructive feedback from others to improve own performance

---

ACCEPTING MISTAKES AS OPPORTUNITIES

Leverages failures as a tool to learn and grow

To wrap up the Learning from Mistakes principle, it's only appropriate that we conclude with the behavior responsible for making learning possible: the choice to *accept mistakes as opportunities.*

To most people most of the time, a mistake is painful. We have been conditioned to feel embarrassed or guilty when we have an accident or make any kind of mistake: "I am upset at myself for letting this happen." Although others sometimes make us feel guilty for our mistakes, we usually punish ourselves worse. Still, the best learners, and the most *resilient* leaders, are the people who keep themselves from being mired in negativity and self-loathing and see the mistakes they make for what they are: opportunities to learn something and improve—even to laugh at oneself.

When it comes to learning from mistakes, here's something we all learned about when we were young: fire. I doubt it's possible to grow up without ever burning yourself, and as you learned at whatever age, it *hurts* to get burned. But as youngsters we're also told, often by our parents, to see the mistake as a learning opportunity. Even as adults we're cautioned that if we play with fire, we'll get burned. The people who can handle fire without burning themselves are the people who have, well, been burned enough times to know better—literally and figuratively.

On the topic of fire—throughout history, lots of people have sought to invent a way to light fires quickly, but modern chemistry took a while to catch up. Not only that, but the match was the result of an accident—someone had bothered to learn from a mistake.

The match, as we know it today, was invented by a chemist named John Walker. There were inventions similar to his "friction match" that had come before it—different kinds of flammable chemicals at the ends of sticks—but none that were reliable, cheap, safe, and easy to use. While experimenting with a new chemical compound, some of it had dried on a wooden stirring stick, and when he tried to scrape it off on the hearth, the compound caught fire and held the flame on its own.

To Walker's credit, he was exhibiting a key leadership attribute before he figured out the match: he was **open to trying new things** and was able to solve an old problem. Walker would never have gotten the idea for the friction match if he hadn't been trying to invent something else; nor would the friction match have succeeded if he weren't willing to duplicate the results of his accident. More acutely, the very factor that defines the usefulness of the friction match—easy lighting by friction—was discovered by mistake. Walker's chance discovery wasn't just one step forward for that invention, it was ***the*** step forward; the match has persisted, virtually unchanged, for almost 200 years after his improvements (except that we've added other inventions like the lighter).

Walker would probably echo the sentiment of Thomas Edison, who, generations later, would insist: "I have not failed. I've just found 10,000 ways that won't work." Except, eventually, both men did find the way that worked for their respective inventions, and we repeat their names because of it. Having a familiarity with mistakes, it turns out, is not a sign of failure or progress in the wrong direction. In the case of effective leaders, it's a sign that they will know their problems better, and as a result, **produce positive results from the mistakes of self and others**, while possessing motivation big enough to continue generating solutions.

Accidental or "mistaken" inventions haven't just been the pyro's delight; such inventions have saved lives, too. By his own account, Sir Alexander Fleming didn't invent penicillin so much as he accidentally discovered it.

In case you didn't know, penicillin is created from a type of mold. One morning in 1928, Fleming entered his lab and saw that a petri dish of bacteria had been left open by a window and was contaminated with a blue-green mold. He noticed, however, that there was a halo of dead bacteria around the mold, which indicated that the bacteria had come into contact with the mold and had been killed. He was able to use this insight to grow more mold and eventually develop the world's first powerful antibiotic, thereby saving millions (if not billions) of lives by his bold discovery.

Imagine how easy it would have been for Fleming to walk into the lab, see the mold contaminating the petri dish with bacteria, and then simply throw it away, concluding the sample was compromised. Fleming's willingness to not only learn from a mistake but examine it much more closely is what accounted for a success greater than anything else upon which he had been working.

Fleming "invented" penicillin because he saw a mistake as an opportunity. His efforts didn't stop with its discovery and invention, however. Fleming was not a good speaker or writer, nor was he well-known in his field. Fleming also **used lessons from mistakes for self-improvement**, not just of his science but also of his own professional tenure; he had to correct his other shortcomings before his invention would see its full usefulness.

Effective leaders **view mistakes as learning opportunities,** however bittersweet, and do not let these mistakes burden their future success. They recognize that failure is leverage, not a load to carry, and that it can be used in surprisingly powerful ways. Comedians, for example, often get good laughs telling stories about how they got started in stand-up—how they were nervous and under-prepared, how they were *not* funny, how they failed hard and managed to laugh about it later. I'd suggest those stories succeed because they're more honest and sincere, because they reveal more about personal failure to us—but in a way that properly makes light of that failure and turns it into eventual success.

Carol Burnett provided a formula: comedy is tragedy plus time. Sure, we can see failures and missed opportunities as "tragedies," and they often feel that way when they've just happened; give them time, however, and they can become something else—the way that a grotesque-looking larva can become a gorgeous butterfly. Often, the people best-suited for leadership are not the "perfect" people but the ones who can accept the imperfections and "tragedies" in their own lives and find humor—the ability to laugh at themselves—or better, the ability to learn from their former weaknesses and failings. Effective leaders are always searching for signs of their own maturation, or at least for the scars they can show to tell a story or make a point.

You may notice that people who have scars to show, and stories to tell about them, aren't usually more fearful of the world for the hurt that it's caused them. If anything, most people are braver for it, and stronger for having survived, and learned, and then told the story. Effective leaders **accept the fact that they are not perfect,** and mistakes are a part of life. Making mistakes may hurt initially, but those making them usually become better people as a result, if they have the will to make the best of each situation and improve themselves wherever they see opportunity. Scars are imperfections, and we all have them; effective leaders will accept their own, laugh about them, learn from them, and become even more effective as a result.

In summary, a leader who accepts mistakes as opportunities . . .

- Views mistakes as learning opportunities
- Is open to trying new things
- Uses lessons from mistakes for self-improvement
- Accepts the fact that he or she is not perfect
- Produces positive results from the mistakes of self and others

SELF-REFLECTION

LEARN FROM MISTAKES

Now that you have more information about some of the behaviors and attributes associated with the Learning from Mistakes principle, take a moment to reflect and rate yourself on your use of them.

INSTRUCTIONS

Read each statement below. **Use the 0–4 scale to rate yourself on how often you use the attribute described.**

0	1	2	3	4
NEVER	**RARELY**	**SOMETIMES**	**HALF THE TIME**	**MOST TIMES**

OPEN TO NEW IDEAS

		YOU
1	Use innovative approaches to solve problems	
2	Are constantly looking for better ways to do things	
3	Demonstrate the capacity to innovate	
4	Generate new ideas by examining issues from different perspectives	
5	Question the status quo to uncover new methods for doing things	

SUBTOTAL SCORE

LEARNS ON THE FLY

		YOU
6	Use a variety of strategies to learn on the job	
7	Quickly develop an understanding of complex situations	
8	Rapidly discover new approaches to doing things	
9	Generate a variety of options to find solutions	
10	Quickly master skills and knowledge required to perform new tasks	
	SUBTOTAL SCORE	

TAKES RISKS

		YOU
11	Often use unconventional approaches to achieve goals	
12	Employ critical thinking skills to help manage risks	
13	Make responsible decisions despite having incomplete information	
14	Demonstrate that risk-taking is a necessary component of success	
15	Welcome the challenge of the unknown	
	SUBTOTAL SCORE	

REFLECTS ON EXPERIENCES

		YOU
16	Leverage your experience to make decisions	
17	Learn from both accomplishments and setbacks	
18	Want to know what went right/wrong and why each occurred	
19	Reflect on the past to envision future possibilities	
20	Use constructive feedback from others to improve own performance	
	SUBTOTAL SCORE	

ACCEPTS MISTAKES AS OPPORTUNITIES

		YOU ⬇
21	View mistakes as learning opportunities	
22	Are open to trying new things	
23	Use lessons from mistakes for self-improvement	
24	Accept the fact that you are not perfect	
25	Produce positive results from the mistakes of self and others	

SUBTOTAL SCORE ➲

± YOUR SCORE FOR THIS PRINCIPLE ±

	BEHAVIOR	SUBTOTAL SCORES
A	OPEN TO NEW IDEAS	
B	LEARNS ON THE FLY	
C	TAKES RISKS	
D	REFLECTS ON EXPERIENCES	
E	ACCEPTS MISTAKES AS OPPORTUNITIES	

TOTAL SCORE ➲

---

79 to 100 (High) — You demonstrate very effective use of this principle. Inspire and help others develop skills to successfully use it.

65 to 78 (Average) — You demonstrate effective use of this principle. Continue working to enhance your ability to use it.

Below 65 (Low) — You demonstrate limited use of this principle. Take advantage of opportunities to enhance your ability to use it.

For a more comprehensive evaluation, a companion 360° assessment (LEAD 360) is available with this book. The assessment allows members of your immediate work circle to assess the degree to which you exhibit the principles and behaviors discussed in this book.

*Visit **www.AlonzoJohnsonPHD.com** or **www.lead360assessment.com** for additional information on how to complete the LEAD 360 assessment.*

PRINCIPLE TWO
EXEMPLIFY COMPETENCE

We have all heard or read stories about supervisors who were not competent in their jobs or positions as leaders. This is the perfect recipe for employee dissatisfaction, disengagement, and turnover in a company. I am fortunate to have known and worked with several leaders who exemplified competence. One of those leaders—let's call him Sam—really stands out because he exuded competence.

My first substantive encounter with Sam was during a leadership workshop, which he led. I remember being impressed with the way he articulated the content of the session and modeled the behavior that he presented. His breadth of knowledge and skills positioned him as an expert on leadership. Sam gained my respect, and I view him as a role model to this day.

Two years after attending that workshop, Sam became my boss. I was excited to work for such a professional. Sam would give me assignments with increasing responsibility, and then coach and mentor me until I was successful. Looking back over the years that I worked for him, Sam epitomized the characteristics of a competent leader.

During the time that I reported to Sam, he made me the benefactor of not only his technical competence but also his knowledge of interpersonal interactions or behavioral competence. Both technical and behavioral competence go hand in hand. Have you ever met someone who was technically competent at performing a task or job but had "no personality," or someone who could sell ice to a polar bear but came up short when it was time to deliver the ice?

Sam had a great balance of both technical and behavioral competence, and because he was a great leader, he took the time to mentor me on finding that balance. In doing so, Sam would provide me with opportunities to demonstrate my technical competence by asking me to present reports to senior leadership. When I had an important meeting with a senior leader, he would offer his perspective on the best approach to take with that leader. He would say, for example: "John is introverted, and you have a preference for extraversion, so don't rush him for a response when you ask a question. Give him a brief moment to think about things before responding."

Or: "Speak up when you meet with Greg. He can smell a timid person from a mile away, so be assertive and you'll earn his respect."

Sam realized that exemplifying technical competence (the "what") alone is not the complete package; he took it a step further by instilling in me how to deliver that competence (the "how").

So, what behaviors do leaders who exemplify competence demonstrate? These leaders...

- ☐ **SET THE EXAMPLE**
- ☐ **DISPLAY EXPERT POWER**
- ☐ **BUILD TRUST**
- ☐ **EXHIBIT A WEALTH OF SKILLS**
- ☐ **ACT AS A SOURCE OF KNOWLEDGE**

Let's explore the second principle for leadership effectiveness, Exemplify Competence, in greater detail. We will start with the *setting the example* behavior.

SETTING THE EXAMPLE

Performs accurately and thoroughly and completes assignments effectively

Effective leaders **demonstrate, in their daily conduct, a commitment to high professional standards,** and they don't willingly allow themselves to operate below those standards. A work environment may set high expectations, but the difference between a good team member and an effective leader is that a good team member will meet the expectations set by others, while the effective leader will exceed or, better, revolutionize those standards with his or her own work. Ironically, many leaders who commit to high professional standards and raise the bar for others don't intend to do so, and in fact many of them weren't in leadership positions in the first place; they were only trying to do the best they could in their role, and they wound up showing their teammates that they, too, could do better.

To refresh an example from the previous section, recall Erin Brockovich, the legal fighter who spearheaded a massive class-action suit without a law degree. As I pointed out before, Erin did not occupy any leadership position at the law firm but was a quick learner and tireless worker. In the middle of the film depiction of her story, Erin is reading printed documents under a small desk lamp; it's dark outside, and the office manager walks down the hall to leave. She stops at Erin's desk, looks down, and says, "You've been reading for hours."

Without looking up, Erin mumbles, "I'm a slow reader."

That response tells us a lot about Erin. Not only was she willing to fill gaps in her knowledge, but she understood why she needed to fill them—and she was **willing to go the extra mile to make sure** that she knew every detail cold. Her poise later in the film's events is owed neither to her judicial talent, nor her education or her experience with the law, because she had none of those. She winds up composed, confident, and fierce because she had invested the time upfront to develop and hone her skills, and in doing so she became an expert on this landmark case—*Anderson, et al. v. Pacific Gas and Electric.*

Effective leaders take these extra steps to make sure that they are better than competent and prepared; effective leaders want to be the consummate experts. When leaders commit to high professional standards, they exude an infectious energy. Other people in the law office picked up on Erin's energy and example, and they all drove harder to successfully resolve the case. Unsurprisingly, the firm saw tremendous growth as a result of the large settlement it earned.

Another of our previous examples—Elon Musk—shares Erin's hunger for information (though he's probably not a slow reader!). He was a precocious learner who seemed to remember everything; when he ran out of books, he began reading the encyclopedia. He swears that he taught himself rocket science just by reading enough. By now he's known as more than a bookworm, but as it was with Erin, his endless reading is a sign of drive and determination that others can now see more readily.

As the principal of three companies, Elon Musk is a busy man, supposedly only managing a few hours' sleep per night. Like Jobs did for Apple, Musk sets very high standards for his teams, often to their dismay and stress—yet his employees consistently explain that it's difficult to feel it's unjust when Musk is right there with them, putting in the same long hours or more. In other words, Musk isn't just **a role model** because of his ambition and success; he's a role model because he *actually models* the behavior that his companies need from their people to succeed, and because he sets expectations at very high, yet reachable levels.

Of course, leading effectively isn't just about knowing the information, nor even about educating others and directing it into practice. Aside from having a wealth of information, leaders also need to display **personal mastery** of the skills that they need to be effective in their role. Effective leaders possess a greater number of skills than people expect. The leader of a band, for example, is responsible for more than knowing how to play his or her instrument. The leader has to be skilled in dealing with equipment, logistics, and money, in addition to managerial, marketing, and administrative skills. (Or be skilled enough to hire talent with expertise in these areas.) A good band makes good music, but a successful band embraces all of these challenges and succeeds at them through its leader.

Take, for example, one of the most successful bands in recent history: the Foo Fighters. The lead singer and rhythm guitarist is Dave Grohl, who started the band after Nirvana (for whom he was drummer) disbanded in 1993. He'd collected a folder of his own songs, so he rented studio time and recorded the material. Here's the catch: *he played every instrument.*

Grohl reflected, in a keynote address to a South by Southwest music festival audience in 2013, how he taught himself to record multi-tracked songs as a kid. He played a song multiple times, each time with a different instrument, while recording it on the tape recorder. Each time, he used the home stereo to play back the song that he'd just recorded, while recording over it (on the tape recorder) with another instrument accompanying. Later in the keynote, he said that this willingness to learn things, to take on all of the band's challenges creatively—everything from management to screening T-shirts—was how he found his place in the music business and ultimately managed to succeed and become an effective band leader.

What leaders like Dave Grohl, Elon Musk, and Erin Brockovich have in common—aside from the ability to live a good example—is a **desire to strive to be the *best*** at what they do. It's important to clarify that, in all three cases, they didn't need to "beat" anyone else to be the best; each of these leaders simply wanted to either make the best music, drive industry in the most positive ways, or bring justice to an unjust situation. What makes them effective leaders is the visibility of their examples, and allowing others to see what they do and learn from it.

In summary, a leader who sets the example . . .

- Demonstrates a commitment to high professional standards
- Goes the extra mile to ensure excellence in his or her work
- Is a role model for others
- Demonstrates personal mastery of the skills of his or her position
- Strives to be the best

DISPLAYING EXPERT POWER

Influences others by demonstrating the skills, knowledge, and abilities of an expert in the field

---

Another behavior of the Exemplifying Competence principle is *displaying expert power*, or the ability to influence others with your expert skills, knowledge, and experience. Effective leaders must know what they're talking about—and what they're doing—to gain the respect and following of others.

Expert power is one of six types of power described by French and Raven in their power taxonomy from their study of social power. While other types of power concern the ability to punish and reward (i.e. coercive and reward powers), establish rights or respect (i.e. legitimate and referent powers), or to act as a resource (i.e. informational power), expert power means that leaders have the ability to influence cooperation and compliance because the people they lead believe they have special knowledge or insights about how to do something.

Thus, the first attribute that we will discuss for expert power is **often knowing the best way to accomplish tasks.** Consider a professional contractor who, in a very literal way, is expected to get things done. To remain competitive and successful, the contractor has to work with subcontractors who frame houses, install fixtures, run wiring, or perform any number of related tasks. The contractor has to know the most cost-effective way to fix problems and work with others to accomplish the task on time and on budget. The sort of person who builds or fixes a house is a good analogy for why leaders need to know what they're doing: if they don't, the house won't get built (or it'll have major problems before long).

Such people may not usually think of themselves as leaders, but they do find themselves in positions of authority above their clients because they know how to do what their clients don't. A normal person might be able to figure out, for example, how to hang a picture frame using whatever means he or she has—but doing it quickly, cost-effectively, without damaging the wall, and in a way that looks good just won't happen if you don't know the best way to hang a picture frame. If you don't know how to do that properly, it doesn't matter how smart you are—and whether you manage to hang it by your own means is missing the point: if you don't know the best way to accomplish that task you've probably wasted time, money and materials, or marred the wall in the process.

In the same way that an experienced contractor knows how to do all things construction and home improvement *correctly through others*, and thus can "lead you to success" for whatever your construction needs are, an effective leader in a corporate or institutional environment knows how to do things correctly within the context of that institution: he or she knows *where* everything is, *who* everyone is and *what* they do, *how* everything works, and *why* things are the way they are. Metaphorically speaking, he or she can build sturdy houses, and then keep those houses in good shape. A leader possessing expert power is able to present logical arguments and supporting evidence to influence others, as well as use his or her credibility and persuasion to get things done. Let's discuss these attributes next.

These attributes of expert power are reminiscent of courtroom strengths—so let's use a courtroom example. In the 1957 film *12 Angry Men*, the twelve jurors at a murder trial retire to their chamber for deliberation, having been told that a guilty verdict will result in a mandatory death sentence. Eleven of the 12 jurors vote *guilty* at the initial count—but Juror 8 (played by Henry Fonda) votes *not guilty*, arguing that the stakes are too high to allow the vote to pass without some discussion.

For the remainder of the film, Juror 8 leads the other jurors through a skeptical examination of the facts: did the young defendant really murder his father? One detail at a time, he slowly unravels the jurors' assumption that the boy had killed his father by pointing out the holes in the prosecution's arguments. He followed this line of thinking not because he was convinced the boy was innocent, or that he was hell-bent on sparing him for some reason, but because he'd been given a specific rule as a juror: to vote *not guilty* if given any reasonable doubt, which he claimed he had.

In this situation, Juror 8 becomes an effective leader by **presenting logical arguments and supporting evidence to influence others.** He doesn't create a reaction in the other jurors by playing to their passions; given the context of the courtroom, he plays upon the facts and reveals how they do or don't support the conclusions the prosecution has reached. By taking an assumption of his own—that the other jurors can, in time, reason with their doubt as he does—he's able to use his logical and moral faculties to become the jurors' source of authority.

Just as important as the ability to use logic as an influencer, effective leaders also need to be able to **use credibility and persuasion to get things done.** In the case of Juror 8, persuasive argumentation is how he managed to lead others, in this case to a different conclusion—but the reason why he was a leader in that situation is that he set himself apart by dissenting first, then used the spotlight to create a tone of reason and cautious disbelief. He was able to drive the discussion because of the precedent he set and maintained. He gained some early converts this way—some jurors switched their votes after examining only one or two pieces of evidence—but even with the stubborn ones, the jurors who held convictions based on other evidence (or even raw prejudices), he eventually won them over by presenting verifiable, factual information in discussions where they could be persuaded. Juror 8's ability to use logic and creditability to persuade the other jurors led to a *not guilty* verdict, acquitting the young defendant of the murder.

Another attribute of expert power is **demonstrating skillful analytical and planning abilities.** One of our nation's favorite historical figures is Ben Franklin. As one token of the respect we afford him, he's the face of the 100-dollar bill, even though he was never President. When we think of the "leaders" of the Founding Fathers, we often think of the more inspirational figures: the towering military leadership of Washington, for instance, or the beautiful rhetoric of Thomas Jefferson. But in the halls of Philadelphia, Franklin was just as important; this was, after all, the city he'd helped plan. This was also the city in which he'd been postmaster for many years, whose improvements to efficiency and planning made the postal service profitable for the first time.

In other words, Franklin was not a public figure or a visionary leader so much as a pragmatist, a planner, and a voice of reason. He was someone who knew how to make things work by planning them carefully or re-examining the details.

Ben Franklin also possessed the fifth attribute of expert power: the **ability to influence others because of expert knowledge.** Just as Franklin was a statesman, writer, and thinker, he was also a scientist and inventor. Not least important, he was a *publisher*—someone who, in the course of his work, is naturally mindful of communicating ideas to people in the best way possible to influence their positions on a variety of topical issues. (No surprise that he was a natural advisor for the drafting of the Declaration of Independence.)

To say the least, Franklin knew a lot about a lot of things, and this earned him a good deal of admiration even in his own time. Though not the boldest and most idealistic of our leaders, he was certainly one of the most practical and knowledgeable; he was the *expert* we needed to help build our nation.

In summary, a leader who displays expert power . . .

- Often knows the best way to accomplish tasks
- Presents logical arguments and supporting evidence to influence others
- Uses his or her credibility and persuasion to get things done
- Demonstrates skillful analytical and planning abilities
- Influences others because of his or her expert knowledge

BUILDING TRUST

Inspires others by being competent and demonstrating the capacity to lead

---

The next behavior that we will discuss for the Exemplify Competence principle is *building trust.* A leader who exemplifies competence will build trust among his or her team members. Building trust involves learning how to attract and inspire others through competence and a demonstrated capacity to lead.

Leaders who build trust have the **capacity to lead effectively in different circumstances.** No one likes a fair-weather leader, and no one respects someone who can inspire only in the best or worst of times. Leaders build trust when they prove that they have ability—which cannot be faked—and when they prove that their ability persists despite challenges, difficulties, and unpredictable circumstances.

Let's consider the global Recession of 2008 when the trust of many leaders came into question. This event created unpredictable circumstances for leaders. Many of them struggled to keep pace with the rapidly changing economy. Their primary tactic for remaining afloat was to lay off scores of employees. Rampant downsizing created a lack of trust among employees, as many wondered whether they would be next to get the axe.

While numerous companies failed as a result of the Recession, those that succeeded did so, in part, because of the ability of their leaders to build trust by effectively leading their employees, even in a shrinking economy. Leading effectively in changing environments requires competence, which not only fosters foresight and flexibility but also allows leaders to inspire employees during difficult times.

Effective leaders **demonstrate the ability to make sound decisions that others trust.** Notice that I did not say "decisions other people like." As countless others have said before, leaders do what's right, not what's popular. An average manager becomes a leader when he or she begins demonstrating the ability to inspire confidence and cooperation, even when making unpopular decisions. And what makes them a trustworthy leader is when others can consistently see the reasoning behind those decisions.

This latter part deserves a bit more attention. Making sound decisions means making decisions that are well-reasoned, that defer to proper authority, that prioritize the biggest problems, and that observe the ultimate goal of a person's leadership ("success" by whatever definition). To exemplify competence is to make decisions supported by honest, logical arguments or reasoning, as I described in the second and third attributes of "displays expert power" earlier in this book.

Effective leaders also have the ability to **inspire trust by demonstrating their competence.** In the television series *M*A*S*H*, the characters are doctors and nurses at a Mobile Army Surgical Hospital (MASH) in South Korea during the Korean War. After their first commander suddenly leaves, the Army appoints Colonel Sherman Potter to take command. The first source of hesitation among the other doctors—all younger, university-trained surgeons—was the belief that Colonel Potter would prove incompetent as a surgeon, being a doctor trained by the Army before the First World War. The second hesitation among the team was that Potter's Regular Army history might clash with the lax style of his predecessor, who—like the other doctors—saw himself more as a doctor in uniform than a military officer.

The chief surgeon of the unit is Hawkeye Pierce. The quality that makes Hawkeye the informal leader of the team is his surgical skill, and it's Hawkeye's observation (and blessing) of Potter's technique that ultimately confirms Potter as the legitimate leader of the unit. In turn, Potter is able to live up to his office as commanding officer and inspire their trust by demonstrating his different competencies to different people—medical competency for the operating room, interpersonal competency for his staff, and military competency for the military personnel and operations.

Another attribute of a leader who builds trust is **knowing his or her limitations and knowing when to ask for help.** A surprising number of self-made millionaires have learning disorders, such as dyslexia. Real estate mogul Barbara Corcoran, a celebrity investor on *Shark Tank*, is an example. By her accounts on the show and elsewhere, dyslexia was a central factor in her lackluster academic performance—but she also describes how limitations like dyslexia can be liberating because they can spur people to see the world (and success) in different ways. By knowing their limitations without shame, people can build different strengths and learn sooner how to deal with natural weaknesses.

The second part of this, of course, is compensating for those weaknesses. Barbara Corcoran admits she's not strong with numbers or organization, both of which are important for running a real estate empire—thus enters Esther Kaplan, Corcoran's longtime business partner. Barbara met Esther when interviewing potential salespeople. Although Esther's quiet demeanor was an obvious mismatch for those positions, Barbara noticed the way Esther pulled information at a moment's notice from neatly-organized tabs in her purse. She knew Esther had exactly the strengths she didn't, so she hired her and wound up partnering with her for decades.

In addition to personal limitations, organizational limitations or constraints are ever-present challenges effective leaders must navigate successfully. Organizational policies and procedures are primary sources of these constraints. To build trust, effective leaders **remain current on policies and procedures relevant to their field,** however technical and boring they might seem. Failure to observe standard policies or procedures can spell doom for an organization.

Let's quickly examine those two component parts: policy and procedure. Policy refers broadly to rules and regulations, including both external policies (such as state and federal laws) and internal policies, while procedure refers to the ways that tasks are completed (which includes knowledge like best practices and standard operating procedures, or SOPs). Effective leaders are informed about both policy and procedure, how they relate to one another, and how they relate to the work at hand.

Take, as a specific example, a business leader charged with hiring new staff members. In our current parlance, that business leader needs to know the policies surrounding hiring—everything from internal company standards to specific legal mandates like Equal Employment Opportunity Commission (EEOC) rules—as well as the procedures surrounding hiring, including all parts of the process from application to job offer. Moreover, he or she must be aware of how the policy informs the procedure—why he or she legally can't ask certain questions, for example, or how the company's values and corporate culture should inform the selection of candidates.

As I describe in (much) greater detail in *Hiring Made Easy as PIE*—a book on exactly that subject—having expertise in all parts of a hiring process makes it possible for you to master the hiring process and to drive the company in meaningful ways. Remaining current in your field is an effective way to retain mastery and build trust as a leader.

In summary, a leader who builds trust . . .

- Has the capacity to lead effectively in different environments
- Makes decisions that are trusted by others
- Inspires trust by demonstrating competence
- Knows his or her limitations and when to ask for help
- Remains current on policies and procedures within his or her profession

---

EXHIBITING A WEALTH OF SKILLS

Highly able performer with broad work experience and capabilities

---

A fourth behavior of exemplifying competence is *exhibiting a wealth of skills*, or proving yourself as a highly able performer with broad experience and capabilities. As I've written before, ability can't be faked; leaders are charged with showing people the right skills, not just sending the right message.

Effective leaders **possess a diverse set of skills.** In other words, they need to have several different skills at a certain degree of mastery, not just one or two. While it's important to have expertise in certain areas, people who have depth of experience without breadth can be limited in their ability to advise and lead others.

Examine any of the examples I've given thus far and you'll notice that none of them—not a single one of those people—is a one-trick pony. If anything, each person has become a jack-of-all-trades, learning the specific details of his or her task but also having some knowledge of other tasks, processes, or the people touching them—and as their knowledge spiders out, they become increasingly well-rounded and insightful leaders by virtue of that aggregate knowledge.

Another attribute of exhibiting a wealth of skills is **consistently demonstrating mastery of tasks.** Consider, for instance, Sir Richard Branson, the founder of Virgin Group. Virgin Group now comprises more than 400 companies, all under a name he created—and supposedly, the name "Virgin" was chosen because, at the time that he and his partners began work, all of them admitted to knowing nothing about business.

Branson began his career in the record business, but only selling records to start. Once he had found a niche and began mastering the sale of others' records, he took an interest in *recording* records, and thus began Virgin Records. When he took an interest in aviation in the 1980s—something completely apart from the music business—he decided to start Virgin Atlantic Airways, which now produces billions in annual revenue. When he took an interest in communications in the 1990s, he founded Virgin Mobile. (And so on.)

The only thing each venture had in common, aside from Branson himself, was Branson's interest in mastering the project (or industry) in front of him. Branson has a deep interest in records, of course, but it wasn't a passion for music that drove him; it was an entrepreneurial passion, something about the business of selling music. First he became skilled at selling records; the next logical step, to him, was to master recording music and then sell it. After that, when the music industry no longer offered challenges he wished to master, he focused his attentions elsewhere. It's made him one of the most recognizable entrepreneurs in the world, and he seems to offer proof of the old saying, *Jack of all trades, master of none, but better than master of one.*

Leaders who exhibit a wealth of skills have **the ability to provide useful input on almost any problem.** This useful input is usually drawn from one or more of the following sources: skills and knowledge, experience, or contextual insight. *Skills and knowledge* is the matter we've been discussing, within the content of the Exemplifying Competence principle, and refers to the abilities a leader can employ right away. *Experience* is the sum of a person's insight from past events; the more time a person has spent fixing problems of a certain type, the more experience he or she will have to leverage. *Contextual insight* is the ability leaders have to put pieces together, whether that means identifying the right experts and tools to fix the problem or even identifying the missing pieces that the team needs to obtain a resolution.

If you don't have skills and knowledge—if you can't do something or don't know how to get something done—there's no faking it. If you don't have experience doing something, there's no replacement for the time it takes to get it. If you can't see the bigger picture or identify how to begin solving certain problems, your leadership effectiveness will be greatly diminished.

If you do have all three sources (skills and knowledge, experience, and contextual insights), you will be able to provide useful input on almost any problem relative to the role you play within your team. You will be able to lead that team because you have the means to flexibly, yet effectively, deal with a variety of problems—because you will have solved similar problems already, or at least you'll be able to understand what's going wrong.

The next attribute that we will discuss for leaders who exhibit a wealth of skills is **becoming the first point of contact for troubleshooting or problem-solving.** There's a good chance that each of you has a real example of your own, so let me ask you a couple of questions. Try to think of a real person as I do.

In your office, place of work, or life in general, is there anyone who seems to know where *everything* is? Is there someone who seems uniquely able to fix problems, like they have a "magic touch" no one else does? Is there someone who automatically makes situations better, just by entering and trying to help? Since you may have a person in mind by now, one final question: *Would everything fall apart if that person suddenly left?*

If you answered *yes* to the final question—or if you had to argue with yourself before saying *no*—that person is a leader, whether they're acknowledged as such or not. In the same way that real competence and skill can't be faked, people who provide real leadership value accrue real leadership potential, especially as everyone becomes aware of how uniquely suited they are to help lead or resolve certain situations.

Effective leaders do one of two things to become this prominent: they consistently connect problems with people who can solve them, or more directly, they become the sorts of people upon whom others rely for excellence.

The final attribute that we will explore for exhibiting a wealth of skills is **drawing on a wide range of work experience.** Most directly, this means applying one's own real and lived experience; there's nothing you understand so intuitively as your own memories, so people with a deeper and more diverse collection of useful experiences are usually better suited as leaders. As we discussed previously, having some breadth of personal experience makes you more self-confident, more adaptable, and generally more capable of solving problems.

However, "drawing on a wide range of experience" isn't limited to drawing from one's own experience. To make the best of any situation, a leader must be aware of the whole team's assets, including their aggregate experiences. The best leaders realize that they must develop others on the team to be leaders and some of their best wisdom comes from others.

Re-examine Richard Branson. In the first place, it's worth noting that he's dyslexic, that he never did have high hopes for an academically charged future. What he relied upon instead were his wide range of personal skills and, especially later, his own personal experiences, along with the skills and experiences of the people who joined him on his ventures. Instead of diving deep and learning everything he could about one or two subjects, Branson took a more scattered approach. He did what his devoted interests and array of tools allowed—and especially as his competence widened, it allowed him to do virtually whatever he wanted to attempt. If you examine his success, he clearly had some expert skills.

In summary, a leader who exhibits a wealth of knowledge . . .

- Possesses a diverse set of skills
- Consistently demonstrates mastery of tasks
- Can provide useful input on almost every problem
- Is the first point of contact for troubleshooting/problem-solving issues
- Draws on a wide range of work experience

ACTS AS A SOURCE OF KNOWLEDGE

Has expert know-how of the profession

The last behavior for exemplifying competence is ***acting** as a source of knowledge*. The previous four behaviors concern how leaders use the knowledge that they have to experiment, fill gaps, develop relationships, and learn practical skills. In this sense, one could say that competence is one's ability to use one's own knowledge (and learning) to effective and practical ends. Acting as a source of knowledge is putting that competence on display, and providing opportunities for effective leadership skills to shine through.

Since others view leaders who are competent as a resource from which to draw, they often serve as a source of knowledge. Two foundational attributes are required in order for leaders to act in such a capacity: **being seen as experts in their field,** and **being known as the go-to person for insight or information about their profession.**

Think back to the first job you ever held. Most likely, when you started, you didn't know how everything worked; you hadn't been trained well enough, if at all, and you didn't yet have a wealth of information accumulated that could help you. Chances are, then, that you looked to someone else. To whom did you turn whenever you had a question or didn't know how to do something? Did you turn to one specific person more than you turned to anyone else? If so, that was your *go-to person*, and there's a good chance that he or she was your leader or someone you saw as a leader.

Go-to people are important because they combine two useful traits: not only are they competent people who have knowledge about something, but they are also helpful people who are willing to share that knowledge. Assuming similar experience and background knowledge, who's the more likely candidate for the go-to person role—Janice, the office manager who smiles, or Caleb, the office manager who becomes impatient when asked too many questions? Janice, of course.

We call them "go-to" people because, well, we habitually go to them for something—but if we consistently go to them, it stands to reason that we also consistently get real answers or help from them. Thus, leaders who act as a source of knowledge:

- **Are considered valuable resources for professional matters**
- **Consistently demonstrate a high level of professional knowledge**
- **Have the know-how to be effective in their positions**

Another characteristic of leaders who act as a source of knowledge possess that brings us back for more is *quality*. If someone gives us good, insightful answers, we are much more likely to ask another question of that person than of someone who gives a short, terse answer or someone who seems uninterested in the subject. People who eventually become experts are knowledgeable people first, and many become experts for the same reasons they were once considered "go-to" people: they *try* to be insightful, and they use their knowledge with the awareness that it has the power to help people. They tend to believe that details and correctness matter in any situation.

This is why when organizations are onboarding new employees, they are often paired with the "star players" of the team. Leaders want the newest, most impressionable employees to be shaped by those who know the most and do their jobs correctly. Leaders recognize that these "star players" consistently demonstrate a higher level of professional knowledge than their peers, and they depend upon them to set high standards for the newcomers.

Let's move beyond being a "go-to" person or someone handy for regular workplace matters. What happens when the team needs more than that—when the situation calls for deeper attention or expertise?

Consider, as an example, the result of an audit and the company is intensely studying some question or trying to fix a problem. Suppose the company observes a major drop in profits, and the leadership doesn't understand why or doesn't know how to fix the problem. The people who step up and make strides towards solving the problem or offer meaningful and actionable insights show the real power of their knowledge. That's the sort of leadership we're discussing here.

Knowledgeable leaders, in situations like these, begin to cross into the realm of true experts. If the person who spoke up worked in logistics and offered good suggestions for cutting costs—suggestions that are practical that the company's leadership had not yet entertained—that person would rightly be anointed an expert. The same would be true of someone who could offer effective, actionable suggestions for increasing sales, or doubling efficiency, or improving employee engagement.

At the end of the day, the main quality that defines an expert leader is simply the desire to do his or her job well, and to help others do the same. To lead effectively through expert knowledge or *act as a source of knowledge* is to begin with the assumption that knowing more than the average Joe Leader and knowing how to leverage that knowledge, will allow one to be more effective than the average Joe Leader.

In summary, a leader who acts as a source of knowledge . . .

- Is seen as an expert in his or her field
- Has the know-how to be effective in his or her profession
- Is the go-to person for information about his or her profession
- Consistently demonstrates a high level of professional knowledge
- Is considered a valuable resource for professional material

SELF-REFLECTION

EXEMPLIFY COMPETENCE

Now that you have more information about some of the behaviors and attributes associated with the Exemplify Competence principle, take a moment to reflect and rate yourself on your use of them.

INSTRUCTIONS

Read each statement below. **Use the 0–4 scale to rate yourself on how often you use the attribute described.**

0	1	2	3	4
NEVER	**RARELY**	**SOMETIMES**	**HALF THE TIME**	**MOST TIMES**

SETS THE EXAMPLE

		YOU
26	Demonstrate a commitment to high professional standards	
27	Go the extra mile to ensure excellence	
28	Are a role model for others	
29	Demonstrate personal mastery of the skills associated with your position	
30	Strive to be the best	
	SUBTOTAL SCORE	

DISPLAYS EXPERT POWER

		YOU
31	Often know the best way to accomplish tasks	
32	Present logical arguments and supporting evidence to influence others	
33	Use your credibility and persuasion to get things done	
34	Demonstrate skillful analytical and planning abilities	
35	Influence others because of your expert knowledge	
	SUBTOTAL SCORE	

BUILDS TRUST

		YOU
36	Have the capacity to lead effectively in different environments	
37	Make decisions that are trusted by others	
38	Inspire trust by demonstrating competence	
39	Know your limitations and when to ask for help	
40	Remain current on policies and procedures within your profession	
	SUBTOTAL SCORE	

EXHIBITS A WEALTH OF SKILLS

		YOU
41	Possess a diverse set of skills	
42	Consistently demonstrate mastery of tasks	
43	Can provide useful input on almost every problem	
44	Are the first point of contact for troubleshooting/problem-solving issues	
45	Draw on a wide range of work experience	
	SUBTOTAL SCORE	

ACTS AS A SOURCE OF KNOWLEDGE

		YOU ➜
46	Are seen as an expert in your field	
47	Have the know-how to be effective in your profession	
48	Are the go-to person for information about your profession	
49	Consistently demonstrate a high level of professional knowledge	
50	Are considered a valuable resource for professional matters	

SUBTOTAL SCORE ➜

± YOUR SCORE FOR THIS PRINCIPLE ±

	BEHAVIOR	SUBTOTAL SCORES
F	SETS THE EXAMPLE	
G	DISPLAYS EXPERT POWER	
H	BUILDS TRUST	
I	EXHIBITS A WEALTH OF SKILLS	
J	ACTS AS A SOURCE OF KNOWLEDGE	

TOTAL SCORE ➜

---

79 to 100 (High) — You demonstrate very effective use of this principle. Inspire and help others develop skills to successfully use it.

65 to 78 (Average) — You demonstrate effective use of this principle. Continue working to enhance your ability to use it.

Below 65 (Low) — You demonstrate limited use of this principle. Take advantage of opportunities to enhance your ability to use it.

For a more comprehensive evaluation, a companion 360° assessment (LEAD 360) is available with this book. The assessment allows members of your immediate work circle to assess the degree to which you exhibit the principles and behaviors discussed in this book.

*Visit **www.AlonzoJohnsonPHD.com** or **www.lead360assessment.com** for additional information on how to complete the LEAD 360 assessment.*

PRINCIPLE THREE
ADD VALUE

When shopping, most of us look for quality products or services that offer more for the money. This is known as *value*. A drive-through car wash in my neighborhood offers self-service pre-wash, detailing, and vacuuming free with the purchase of a car wash. You would need to scrounge up a fistful of quarters to get these accoutrements at other car washes, but this wash provides them as added value.

In addition to looking for value when shopping, many of us strive to add value to those around us and to the organization in which we work. We add value extrinsically or intrinsically. This is especially true if we are leaders.

For example, my first job in the private sector was performing dual roles of quality manager and training manager. I oversaw continuous improvement initiatives for two manufacturing facilities, in addition to developing and conducting training programs on quality and other related subjects.

The state in which the two production facilities were located offered an economic incentive to companies that provided specific skills training to residents employed at the company. This incentive was a corporate tax credit, valued up to $100,000 annually. It was a challenging process to complete and submit the application along with supporting documentation to get the tax credit approved.

I took on this project of earning a tax credit for my company. Over time, it became an annual challenge of sorts—to try to return as much funding to the training budget as possible to offset our training cost. My efforts paid off. For several years, I earned tax credits that were greater than our training budget; some years, I earned tax credits that exceeded my annual salary—both are great examples of adding an extrinsic financial value.

How about an example highlighting added intrinsic value? Let's discuss a service learning project in which I was involved. *Service-learning* is a teaching strategy in which students provide a service to the community as part of the requirement of their program of study. While working as a college professor, I assigned students in one of my classes a service-learning project. The service-learning project was a response to concerns that several local business owners had shared with college faculty; they felt that students who had recently graduated and entered the workforce lacked workplace readiness skills. The newly minted employees had the prerequisite academic skills but many of them lacked the problem-solving, teamwork, and interpersonal communication skills required for many entry level positions.

To address the problem and add value to the business owners (and students), I assigned a capstone assignment in one of the college classes that I taught, as part of the service learning project. The assignment required students to use the skills that they had learned in my class to conduct training sessions for local high school students. The topics of the sessions included problem solving, team building, conflict management, effective communication, and change management.

The project was successful. It added value to the students in my class by providing training experience. It also added value to the high school students receiving the training, as well as to their high schools. And because the project addressed concerns from some of the local business owners, it added value to them and the broader community.

Adding value means making things or people better than when you found it or them. There are many ways to add value. In what ways have you added value recently at work or at home?

Below is a list of behaviors that you'll often see exhibited by a leader who adds value:

- ☐ **GOES BEYOND WHAT IS EXPECTED**
- ☐ **SHARES KNOWLEDGE AND RESOURCES FREELY**
- ☐ **EXHIBITS A PERSONAL LEADERSHIP BRAND**
- ☐ **DISPLAYS RESILIENCE**
- ☐ **STAYS RELEVANT**

GOING BEYOND WHAT IS EXPECTED

Pushes the limits and constantly delivers exceptional performance

---

The first behavior that we will discuss for the Adding Value principle is *going beyond what is expected.* Effective leaders don't just do their jobs and perform to standards, they constantly **push the limits of what is expected** and go beyond them. Exceptional performance is their hallmark, and they **consistently deliver more than what is expected or required.**

For centuries, leaders have been excelling by consistently demonstrating these behaviors. Florence Nightingale, a social activist, statistician, and the founder of modern nursing, perfectly exemplified these leadership attributes. Nightingale came to prominence after volunteering to train and lead a team of nurses to treat wounded soldiers during the Crimean War between 1853 and 1856. Upon arriving at the British medical facility, she found the healthcare provided to the wounded deplorable. Critical medical supplies were low; hygiene was being neglected; and the facility was overcrowded, poorly ventilated, and had malfunctioning sewer systems. These conditions fueled illnesses such as typhus, typhoid, cholera, and dysentery.

Serious infections were commonplace, and more soldiers died from diseases than from battle wounds.

Nightingale embraced this assignment and added value through her exemplary work improving these conditions. To improve the quality of care for the wounded, she pioneered healthcare processes that had never been considered before in a wartime hospital environment. She implemented good hygiene practices and improved unsanitary conditions. According to some accounts, Nightingale's efforts reduced the death rates of wounded soldiers from 42% to 2%—an amazing statistic even to this day. After the war, Nightingale continued exceeding expectations. She devised and implemented statistical methods to analyze and improve nursing services and patient treatment processes, as well as healthy living habits for the general public.

Among the many examples of this type of value-added leadership in modern day business environments—leaders who demonstrate grit by pushing the limits and consistently delivering positively unexpected results—is Indra Nooyi, Chairman and CEO of PepsiCo. Since Nooyi took the leadership helm in 2001, she has proven herself to be a visionary and has delivered more value to customers and shareholders than anticipated. Years ago, Nooyi envisioned a world in which consumers would opt for healthier alternatives than the sugar-laden flagship product, Pepsi Cola. Whether or not you are a Pepsi brand enthusiast, Nooyi led the company through the reformulation of some brands to be healthier, and she launched sustainability initiatives to lessen the company's impact on the environment, all while delivering high returns to shareholders.

In her quest to push the limits without alienating any consumer segments, Nooyi reclassified PepsiCo's products into three categories: "fun for you" (regular sodas, potato chips, etc.), "better for you" (diet and low-fat sodas and snacks), and "good for you" (items such as oatmeal). She funded each category according to her focus on healthy living, ensuring that the healthier products received the larger budget. Nooyi vowed to improve the healthiness of products in the "fun" category as well. This bold decision to focus energies and other resources on healthier alternatives has kept PepsiCo as a fierce competitor to Coca-Cola. As of 2015, the sale of healthier PepsiCo products has overtaken that of Coca-Cola.

Nooyi did not stop there. (We talked about consistently delivering more than expected, right?) She implemented environmental sustainability initiatives throughout the company. These initiatives included reducing the amount of water used in production, recycling waste, and using alternative fuels and electric vehicles for the delivery fleet. Between 2010 and 2015, those initiatives resulted in more than $375 million in estimated cost savings.

As Nooyi continues to lead PepsiCo, she has consistently delivered more than expected in both the organic growth of the company and its profitability. By introducing the customer design experience concept, Nooyi was able to transform PepsiCo's customers' experience—from the conception and production of the product, to its shelf presence, to how customers will interact with it. This concept has led to growth through innovations and products that customers want. Under Nooyi's leadership, PepsiCo's shareholders earned an 8.9% annual return on their investment between 2004 and 2014.

The story of Indra Nooyi is one of many. Leaders who go beyond what is expected are often **perceived by others as above-average performers.** Let's face it: the perceptions that others have of us (as leaders) are important for a number of reasons; let's review three of them. First, perceptions are a reflection of our personal leadership brand. (We'll discuss personal leadership brand in detail later in this section.) Secondly, our ability to influence others is often based on their perceptions of us. Leaders naturally influence others—some for the right or wrong reason. And finally, being viewed as a leader who is known for making everyone and everything better when he or she is around—adding value—enhances your effectiveness as a leader.

Effective leaders also seem to **gain satisfaction from providing exceptional service to others.** Whether contributing to individuals, organizations, or broader communities, they have an intrinsic desire to give back to something bigger than themselves. Let's go back to the two distinguished leaders we discussed in this section of the book. Florence Nightingale is known in the history books for her strong leadership skills as an adult. She grew up in an affluent home and wanted to be a nurse from an early age. Her parents disapproved of the nursing profession because in those days, it was not a respected career for a woman of her pedigree. Even so, Nightingale said that she had a calling to serve others; the humanitarian services that she provided, especially in nursing, allowed her to fulfill that calling. Florence Nightingale's ability to add exceptional value to the nursing profession has helped shape the nursing profession we know today.

In a similar fashion, Indra Nooyi's desire to make the usual chips, snack foods, and sodas healthier was apparent at the start of her tenure with PepsiCo. At the risk of bankrupting the company, she acknowledged that junk food was unhealthy, took actions to make them healthier, where possible, and started placing more focus on the healthier snacks. Shoppers have rewarded her efforts with increasing revenues over the last several years. With Nooyi guiding one of the biggest companies in the world to focus on the customer's experience, she has continued to deliver exceptional value to customers and shareholders alike.

Leaders who go beyond what is expected never seem to be satisfied with their own performance. They **always see room for improvement,** and take every opportunity to grow personally and professionally. Many leaders find that improving in three essential areas—*communication*, *trust*, and *engagement*—enhances their ability to deliver exceptional performance even more. Let's spend some time discussing these three areas.

COMMUNICATION

Communication is a critical element of effective leadership. It is essential for productivity, and it is key for building good relationships with others. You should make every effort to communicate with members of your team on a regular basis, and promote open communication throughout your team.

Face-to-face communication offers the greatest effectiveness, but email, phone, Skype, or other available technology can get the job done when face-to-face is not possible. The important point is for you to keep the people you lead informed, and be accessible to them when they need you.

TRUST

We discussed trust earlier in the book. Trust has been described as the glue that holds an organization together. The ability to inspire trust affects your influence as a leader, and impacts your organization more than anything else. Trust is an absolute requirement for leadership effectiveness, and you should work towards building it every day by building or enhancing your interpersonal relationships with others. Fostering open communication, showing authenticity, and being supportive of others are a few ways in which you can build or maintain trusting relationships.

ENGAGEMENT

Within the context of effective leadership, engagement is the emotional commitment that you and your team members have towards the organization and its goals. Engaged employees don't just come to work for a salary or promotion. They care about the organization, and come to work motivated to help the organization achieve its goals. Articulating a clear vision to your team members and making sure they are working towards SMART goals (**S**pecific, **M**easurable, **A**chievable, **R**elevant, and **T**imely) that are aligned with organizational strategies are sure ways of enhancing employee engagement.

In summary, a leader who goes beyond what is expected . . .

- Consistently delivers more than what is expected or required
- Is perceived by others as an above-average performer
- Gains satisfaction from providing exceptional service to others
- Pushes the limits of what is expected
- Always sees room for improvement

SHARING KNOWLEDGE AND RESOURCES FREELY

Looks out for others unselfishly

Another behavior for adding value is *sharing knowledge and resources freely*, or looking out for others unselfishly. Leaders who add value not only exhibit selflessness, but they also inspire teamwork and lay the foundation for employee engagement. Another attribute shared by selfless leaders is their willingness to **demonstrate knowledge and skills for others to learn.** They show commitment to developing people, and conscientiously model the skills, knowledge, and behaviors necessary for their success.

The leadership of Mahatma Gandhi, a lawyer and human rights activist, exemplifies the attributes described so far in this section. His first assignment after law school was in South Africa. With a desire to add value by serving others, he worked as a lawyer helping his fellow Indians in their struggle against discrimination. He later continued to fight for social justice in India by leading several social justice campaigns.

Gandhi taught his followers the principles of nonviolent protest by first demonstrating them himself. His selfless leadership resulted in social justice gains in South Africa, and the eventual independence of India in 1947. His demonstrated knowledge and skills as a nonviolent leader also inspired future social activists around the world, including Dr. Martin Luther King, Jr. and Nelson Mandela.

Abraham Maslow put it best when he said, "If we are not modeling what we're teaching, then we are teaching something else." Leaders who demonstrate knowledge and skills for others to learn epitomize what it means to truly add value.

In addition to role modeling to teach and set the example for others, effective leaders add value by **documenting and sharing knowledge gained from past experiences, including mistakes.** Remember our discussion earlier about learning from mistakes? General H. Norman Schwarzkopf followed this practice during the 1991 Gulf War called Operation Desert Storm. His leadership philosophy was shaped by his earlier experiences in Vietnam. He was assigned there twice, once as a Captain in 1965, and again as a Lieutenant Colonel in 1969. During these assignments, young Schwarzkopf observed a flagrant lack of effective leadership skills among his peers and superiors. He noticed that many US Army leaders in Vietnam had low performance standards. They were often afraid to make mistakes, and too careful to be effective leaders. What's more, they did not take care of their soldiers and were infamous for consistently leading from the rear.

As a member of the command group responsible for the invasion of Grenada in 1983, Schwarzkopf continued to learn from his experience. Although successful, the invasion was plagued with logistical problems, as well as poor communication and cooperation among forces of the different branches of the military that were involved in the mission.

Schwarzkopf learned from these mistakes, and when he was charged with the responsibility to lead a multi-national coalition during Operation Desert Storm, he implemented changes based on the lessons he learned from the mistakes in his past. He documented and shared his knowledge with others to ensure that the mistakes that were made in Vietnam and Grenada were not repeated in Operation Desert Storm. Most notably, Schwarzkopf required high standards from everyone, including himself. He took risks and led from the front. He also looked after the soldiers in his command by providing them with emotional and physical support, and while enduring the same hardships as they did, he motivated and inspired them to achieve excellence.

As discussed in the Learning from Mistakes principle, reflecting on experiences is an effective exercise that leaders (in any organization) can use to learn from their experience and document their knowledge in order to transfer it to others.

Unselfishly counseling team members on the best approach to accomplish tasks is another attribute of leaders who share their knowledge and resources freely. Competent leaders are able to advise others concerning best practices and are usually more than happy to make them benefactors of their competence, rather than hoarding their knowledge and resources.

By looking out for their team members in this way, leaders show empathy that builds positive relationships and engagement. And they are role models to those who are aspiring to develop their own leadership skills.

Leaders who look out for others unselfishly **can be counted on to come through for others when needed.** Both Gandhi and General Schwarzkopf came through for others by sharing unselfishly and being there physically and emotionally with their teams. They were not discouraged by hardships but rather leveraged them to first become better people themselves, and then make the lives of those around them better.

According to Robert Greenleaf, a leader whose main concern is for the growth and betterment of others is known as a *servant-leader*. Servant-leaders always use their influence to help those around them grow as a means of growing their broader community.

Do you freely share your knowledge and resources with others? Are you a servant-leader?

When help is required beyond the scope of just sharing knowledge and resources, leaders who add value also have the ability to **provide technical assistance to others.** There are many ways in which leaders can provide technical assistance. Among them include leading a project team, and serving as an internal consultant.

Leading a project team can be a challenging but rewarding experience. Fulfilling such a role allows a leader to add value by offering technical assistance to help the team tackle complex problems. Project team leaders use their expertise to influence all aspects of the project—team charter, technical and people processes, as well as budget. Although they are responsible for actions resulting from their leadership, effective project team leaders are aware that success is only achieved by the contributions of everyone. They not only share their knowledge, but they also share credit for success with their team members.

Let's talk about leaders as *internal consultants*. The concept of organizations using internal consultants has become a popular trend, and this can often be more beneficial than retaining external consultants. Internal consultants offer the benefit of cost savings by getting things done using organic resources. And since they already know the lay of the land, and have well-established relationships, they are usually more efficient than external consultants.

A skilled internal consultant is self-aware, tolerant of ambiguity, has excellent interpersonal and communication skills, and has a knack for facilitating change. Some initiatives within organizations that are prime targets for leaders to offer their expertise are change management, continuous improvement, safety, training, and acquisition and integration of resources.

Effective leaders find ways to share their knowledge and resources with others, so they are keen to leverage their ability to function as internal consultants. Their aim is to add value to help people grow and position their organizations for future success.

In summary, a leader who shares knowledge and resources freely . . .

- Unselfishly counsels team members on best approaches to accomplish tasks
- Documents and shares knowledge gained from past experiences, including mistakes
- Can be counted on to come through for others when needed
- Demonstrates knowledge and skills for others to learn
- Provides technical assistance to others

EXHIBITING A PERSONAL LEADERSHIP BRAND

Demonstrates authenticity and consistency

Exhibiting a personal leadership brand is another behavior that leaders use to add value. Leaders who demonstrate this behavior are well-positioned to add value to those around them and their organizations. And since value is in the eyes of the beholder, a leader's personal brand should exhibit value that is beneficial to those receiving it. Effective leaders exhibit the value they offer to others through their personal strengths. Examples of these strengths include their competence, consistency, self-awareness, and authenticity. Their strengths echo their identity and reinforce their reputation, which casts them as renowned performers within the environment in which they function.

In other words, leaders who exhibit a personal brand **are known for a particular style of leadership** because they **demonstrate leadership traits that are unique to them.** Since people are more comfortable working with those who are familiar to them, these characteristics offer others the advantage of knowing what to expect when working with leaders with a personal brand.

Dr. Martin Luther King, Jr.—a minister, nonviolent civil rights leader, and Nobel Peace Prize recipient—is a great example of a leader who demonstrated a personal leadership brand. He was known for helping others achieve social justice through nonviolent means—a particular style of leadership. Even today, decades after his assassination, the word *nonviolence* is synonymous with his name—a classic example of personal branding.

Another characteristic of leaders who possess and exhibit a personal brand is **consistency in their approach to leadership.** Consistency is an important trait for effective leaders to have because it helps them establish a reputation and causes others to see them as dependable. For employees to have confidence in their leaders, they must be consistent in their responsiveness, support, and the way they lead. When employees don't have confidence in their leader's consistency, they will likely look elsewhere for leadership, which sometimes means leaving the organization.

While consistency creates confidence in leaders and helps to establish their reputation, effective leaders display **genuineness in their interactions with others,** which helps to build trusting relationships. Effective leaders are transparent and authentic in their interactions. They openly and respectfully share their thoughts and beliefs with others, and don't have hidden agendas. Employees who work with authentic leaders don't have to worry about *covering their rears*, because they know that their leaders have their backs.

In addition to having a unique leadership style, Dr. King demonstrated consistency and authenticity throughout his tenure as a civil rights activist. He worked tirelessly for the cause that he was most passionate about—the civil rights of all mankind—and because of it, he was sought after by scores of civil rights groups to help lead their causes. And his authenticity made him approachable for these groups to do so. Dr. King was also known as a great orator, and his consistency and authenticity are still evident in the many speeches found in the King Center's archives.

Authenticity is especially important for building and maintaining a personal brand; there has been evidence of this for ages. In Act 1, Scene III of William Shakespeare's famous tragedy *Hamlet*, Polonius admonishes his son, Laertes, to be true to himself as he is preparing to depart for Paris. He said, "This above all: to thine own self be true, And it must follow, as the night the day, Thou canst not then be false to any man."

Although there are several interpretations about what Polonius meant, the most popular interpretation of the statement today is that he wanted Laertes to be authentic more than everything else.

Leaders develop authenticity by **becoming aware of their strengths, weaknesses, and emotions.** Self-awareness serves to shape other strengths, such as authenticity and consistency, that make up a leader's personal brand.

An ancient Greek maxim urges us to "know thyself." The axiom means to be self-aware beyond knowing your favorite color or music. It means to know who you are within, at your very core. Understanding your personality is an excellent starting point for knowing yourself. According to Duane Schultz and Sydney Schultz, authors of *Theories of Personalities*, *personality* is the enduring characteristics of a person that influence his or her behavior in various situations. Therefore, leaders who understand their personality know their temperament and are better prepared to interact with those around them who are different.

There are myriads of psychometrics available to help leaders assess their personality. Among them are the Myers Briggs Type Indicator® (MBTI®) and the Fundamental Interpersonal Relationship Orientation-Element Behavior™ (FIRO-Element B™). Each of them assesses personality from a different perspective and provides a unique vantage point for self-awareness.

For example, the MBTI® assesses four aspects of personality: where individuals get their energy—externally or internally; how they perceive the world around them—sensory or imagination; how they judge the world around them—logic or values based; and how they live in the world—rigid or flexible.

On the other hand, the FIRO Element B™ assesses three dimensions of interpersonal interactions:

- **Inclusion**—refers to the degree of participation, belongingness and togetherness that an individual wants. The scale measures the degree of interaction that an individual expresses toward others, gets from others, as well as what the individual wants to express and get.
- **Control**— refers to power, decision making and leadership. The scale measures the degree of influence that an individual expresses toward others, gets from others, as well as what the individual wants to express and get.
- **Openness**— refers to sharing personal feelings, friendship and affection with others. The scale measures the degree of closeness that an individual expresses toward others, gets from others, as well as what the individual wants to express and get.

Emotional intelligence, the ability to perceive, express, and control one's emotions during interpersonal interactions and cope with one's environment, provides yet another vantage point for self-awareness.

Research and recent trends show that a high level of emotional intelligence not only leads to self-awareness, but also to greater effectiveness and success as a leader. As with personality, there are many psychometrics that can be used to assess emotional intelligence. The Emotional Quotient Inventory 2.0 (EQ-i 2.0) uses five scales, each with three subscales, to measure an individual's emotional intelligence.

- **Self-Perception** — understanding one's strength and limitations; subscales consist of self-regard, self-actualization, and emotional self-awareness.
- **Self-Expression** — expressing one's emotions; subscales consist of emotional expression, assertiveness, and independence.
- **Interpersonal** — developing and maintaining relationships; subscales consist of interpersonal relationships, empathy, and social responsibility.

- **Decision-Making** — using emotional information to guide decisions; subscales consist of problem solving, reality testing, and impulse control.
- **Stress Management** — coping with one's environment; subscales consist of flexibility, stress tolerance, and optimism.

As stated before, self-awareness is a prerequisite for authenticity. Assessments, such as those named in this section, are useful tools for building self-awareness to both frame and build your personal leadership brand.

So it goes without saying that leaders are not born with a personal brand. In addition to self-awareness, life events help shape their brand over time. Dr. King, for example, wasn't born a great civil rights leader but developed a passion for the cause over his lifetime. His passion was undoubtedly shaped by growing up in the segregated South, and his nonviolent approach was inspired by Mahatma Gandhi. He referred to Gandhi as a guiding light for the nonviolent movement for social change and actually sojourned in India to meet Gandhi's followers early in his career. Dr. King's visit to India resulted in a sharpened commitment to nonviolent principles.

As Dr. King and other leaders (such as Richard Branson and Steve Jobs) developed their personal brands over time, you too, should continue to build the reputation that exhibits who you are. Do so by examining your strengths and weaknesses often—you are a complex human being; being self-aware is a never ending journey. Then leverage the strengths that you have identified to enhance your consistency. Above all, be authentic.

Good or bad, you demonstrate your personal leadership brand every day by behaving the way that you do. Effective leaders are ever mindful of their brand and how it is perceived by others.

In summary, a leader who exhibits a personal leadership brand . . .

- Shows consistency in his or her approach to leadership
- Is aware of his or her strengths, weaknesses, and emotions
- Is genuine in his or her interactions with others
- Is known for a particular style of leadership
- Demonstrates leadership traits that are unique to him or her

---

DISPLAYING RESILIENCE

Is emotionally and physically tough and quickly bounces back from failures

---

Let's discuss why *displaying resilience* is an important behavior for those who add value. If you are a leader, you can expect to encounter setbacks, such as highly stressful situations, illnesses, and sometimes failures. Resilience will be required for you to rebound from these setbacks, to maintain your effectiveness as a leader and add value to your team and your organization. In other words, you'll have to shake it off and step up.

The fable of "The Donkey in the Well" is an example of shaking it off and stepping up as a result of being resilient. Let's spend a little time with this story.

One day a farmer's donkey fell into a well. The animal cried frantically as the farmer figured out what to do. Finally, the farmer concluded that the animal was old, and the well needed to be filled anyway. Neither the well nor the donkey was worth saving.

So the farmer asked his neighbors to help him fill the well. They all grabbed shovels and began shoveling dirt into the well. When the donkey realized what was happening, he became hysterical and brayed pitifully.

Then, after several shovel loads of dirt, the donkey quieted down. When the shovelers looked down into the well, they were amazed at what they saw. As each shovel of dirt fell onto the donkey's back, he would shake it off and take a step up.

As the shovelers continued to toss dirt into the well, the donkey would shake it off and take a step up. To everyone's amazement, the donkey was soon able to step out of the well and trot away!

The moral of this story is when you fall, and life throws dirt at you, shake it off and step up. Just like the donkey that fell into the well, effective leaders **possess the ability to bounce back from past mistakes** because they **demonstrate a high level of stress-tolerance.**

Stress-tolerance appears to be a major enabler for resilience. Dr. Henry Thompson, author of *The Stress Effect*, identified seven best practices for building and maintaining stress-tolerance: **A**wareness, **R**est, **S**upport, **E**xercise, **N**utrition, **A**ttitude, and **L**earning. These best-practice elements form the acronym ARSENAL, and Dr. Thompson suggests that when the elements are employed collectively, they are, indeed, an effective arsenal against stress. Let's briefly explore each best practice element, according to Dr. Thompson.

Awareness — being tuned in to your behavior and knowing what makes you tick. It is the foundation of the other best practice elements.

Rest — rejuvenates your mind and body and is vital for a healthy lifestyle and stress resilience.

Support — having others in your life who provide psychological, emotional, and physical help to both challenge and encourage you to be your best.

Exercise — physical activities that enhance or maintain your physical fitness. A workout routine and maintaining an active lifestyle will result in a high level of stress-tolerance.

Nutrition — receiving the food required for physical/mental health and growth.

Attitude — having a positive outlook towards others and towards life in general.

Learning — continuing to acquire or expand your skills and knowledge. Challenge yourself to grow mentally beyond what you thought was possible. Foster relationships with those who know more than you.

Remember our earlier discussion about self-awareness? Through his research, Dr. Thompson has found that awareness forms the basis for all the other best practice elements. Awareness of self has long been touted as an important factor of emotional intelligence, which supports resilience.

We also discussed emotional intelligence earlier. High emotional intelligence not only enhances self-awareness but also increases *stress-tolerance*, *flexibility*, and *optimism*. These three important factors are used on the Emotional Quotient Inventory 2.0 (EQ-i 2.0) to measure a person's ability to manage stress.

A closer look at each factor illustrates why they are important for building resilience.

Stress-Tolerance is your ability to endure hardships and setbacks, as well as believing that you can impact stressful situations positively.

Flexibility is adjusting your emotions, thoughts, and behaviors to compensate for changing or unpredictable conditions.

Optimism is your outlook on life and ability to remain hopeful, even in the face of adversity.

You may have concluded, from reviewing Dr. Thompson's ARSENAL for managing stress, that a leader's ability to tolerate stress is also due, in part, to his or her level of **physical and mental fitness.**

Jim Loehr and Tony Schwartz, authors of *The Makings of a Corporate Athlete*, suggest that a leader's physical energy is the foundation for three other important energy levels: emotional, mental, and spiritual. They suggest that one energy level builds upon the other, but all of them work in a holistic way to enable leaders to be resilient. For example, intense exercise can produce a feeling of emotional well-being, creating enhanced mental energy. And our spiritual energy provides purpose that motivates us to endure. One of the leadership effectiveness principles of this book is Exemplifying Competence; it's not enough to be competent in your profession; you must be able to maximize each level of energy to sustain leadership effectiveness.

Another factor of resilience is the drive to stay the course. Resilient leaders **demonstrate a tenacious resolve to stay the course, especially in the face of adversity.** And when they fail, they **hold themselves accountable for recovering from mistakes.**

There have been many leaders throughout history who have modeled these characteristics of resilience. One example of such a leader is Walt Disney. Walt suffered setback after setback throughout his career. A newspaper editor fired him, citing, "he lacked imagination and had no good ideas." He started a number of businesses that failed and ended in bankruptcy. At one point in his career, he ate dog food to survive. However, his tenacious resolve to stay the course paid off.

Walt Disney did not blame anyone for his failures. Today, the Disney Company makes billions of dollars from merchandise and movies. There are likely few people throughout the world who are not familiar with at least one of the Disney characters or movies. And Disney theme parks around the world are a popular vacation destination for millions.

In summary, a leader who displays resilience . . .

- Demonstrates a high level of stress-tolerance
- Holds himself or herself accountable for recovering from mistakes
- Maintains his or her physical and mental fitness
- Possesses the ability to bounce back from past mistakes
- Demonstrates a tenacious resolve to stay the course, especially in the face of adversity

---

STAYING RELEVANT

Remains effective by keeping self and the organization current

---

The final behavior that we will discuss for the Adding Value principle is *staying relevant.* To sustain the ability to add value to those around them and their organization, leaders must remain relevant. One practice that effective leaders use to remain relevant is to **regularly evaluate their professional competence. Seeking feedback for self-improvement** is an effective approach to evaluating competence. Feedback can be obtained using a formal method, such as a 360° assessment, or an informal method, such as a face-to-face conversation with someone about your performance. Each of these methods has its advantages and disadvantages.

The 360° assessment (such as the LEAD 360° offered as a companion assessment with this book) provides anonymous feedback from multiple raters such as a boss, direct reports, peers, and sometimes other colleagues, associates, and customers. As its name implies, it provides the leader with full-circle feedback that is more comprehensive than face-to-face feedback from a single source. However, the 360° assessment is more time consuming than face-to-face feedback, since it is completed by multiple raters.

Face-to-face feedback can be obtained directly from someone who has observed your performance, such as a boss, peer, direct report, or customer, and can be provided any time. The benefit that face-to-face feedback has over the 360° assessment is that it is more personal, lets the leader know what's expected of him or her, and provides actionable information that he or she can use right away to improve performance. Face-to-face feedback also contributes to building a culture in which giving and receiving feedback is routine—it builds trust and increases the leader's self-awareness. A major disadvantage of face-to-face feedback is that the person giving it may find it difficult to be candid, especially if the culture doesn't support honest communication.

When asking for face-to-face feedback, let the person from whom you are seeking feedback know, in advance, the specific areas in which you would like to receive the feedback. Advance notice allows the person providing feedback time to prepare, and the specifics help him or her focus the preparation efforts.

When receiving face-to-face feedback, ask open-ended questions to get the conversation going and to clarify discussion points during the conversation. Open-ended questions often begin with "what," "why," or "how," and will often yield complete and meaningful responses, since they often can't be answered with a simple "yes" or "no."

For example, a few good open-ended questions to get a face-to-face feedback session started are as follows:

- In terms of my behavior, what should I start, stop, and continue doing?
- Why do you think my efforts failed?
- What do I need to do more of, and less of?
- How would you handle this problem if you were me?
- What do I need to do to be successful next time, and how should I do it?

In addition to seeking feedback for self-improvement, effective leaders also remain relevant by **understanding how they impact the future of the**

organization. They realize that by **staying abreast of evolving demands and changing accordingly**, they can positively impact the future of the organization. Conversely, not keeping track of these changes (new workplace and consumer trends) will likely erode their effectiveness as leaders, which can lead to the demise of their organization. There is a plethora of well-known companies that were profitable in their heyday, that are now either woefully diminished or no longer exist today. Among them are Blockbuster Videos, Circuit City, and Pan Am Airlines.

Blockbuster, for example, had the opportunity to purchase Netflix on more than one occasion. The leadership team at Blockbuster didn't sense the changing trend in how customers were starting to watch movies—from DVD to online streaming. What's more, the company didn't even secure its own video streaming options the way that Netflix and Redbox did. Simply put, Blockbuster's leaders were not aware of, or did not take seriously, the changes in their environment, and now others are learning from that company's mistakes.

To illustrate why leaders should continuously scan their environments to identify change, let's reflect on the story of the boiling frog. As the story goes, a 19th century researcher placed a frog into a pan of boiling water to determine how it would react to the temperature—it jumped out quickly. He then placed the frog into a pan of cold water and gradually increased the temperature over time. The frog did not sense the gradually increasing temperature and boiled to death. The hypothesis of the experiment was that a cold blooded animal's body temperature would go up and down with the temperature of its environment, and gradual changes would go unnoticed.

Although the results of the experiment have been challenged by later researchers, the story offers a good metaphor for the necessity of leaders to stay abreast of changes in their environments, even small changes.

A SWOT analysis is a useful tool that leaders can use to help scan their environment, and it can be applied at both the individual and organizational levels. SWOT is an acronym that means **S**trengths, **W**eaknesses, **O**pportunities, and **T**hreats. It is used to scan both internal and external environments, thereby identifying internal strengths and weakness, as well as external opportunities and threats.

An example of a SWOT analysis for a consulting business is below.

	HELPFUL	HARMFUL
INTERNAL	**STRENGTHS** Customer Relationships Consistent Quality Solid Expertise Market Agility	**WEAKNESSES** Limited Strategic Business Relationships New Customer Acquisition Lack of Funding Marketing
EXTERNAL	**OPPORTUNITIES** Memberships in Professional Orgs Developing & Leveraging Networks Publishing Books & Resources Presenting at Conferences	**THREATS** Competition from larger consulting firms

As stated earlier, effective leaders **look ahead to their future and the future of the organization.** Hiring great talent is one of the most important tasks that leaders perform to ensure the organization's future. When selecting the best-fit employee, leaders should focus on assessing three important areas—the "Can," the "Will," and the "Fit." They should devote the time necessary to assess these areas by seeking answers to three main questions:

1. **Can the candidate do the job (the "Can")?** Does the candidate have the required skills, knowledge, education, and experience for this position? Is he or she able to articulate real experiences and information to demonstrate that he or she can do the job?

2. **Will the candidate do the job (the "Will")?** Is the candidate motivated to do the job? Are job requirements consistent with what the candidate enjoys doing? Do the career objectives of this person align with the duties of the job, or are there advancement opportunities for him or her? Does the candidate's job history show the type of upward advancement you would expect of him or her?

3. **Is the candidate a good fit for the culture within the organization (the "Fit")?** Does the candidate's work behavior, style, and personality mesh with the job and the company? Will the candidate's level of assertiveness, stress tolerance, and interpersonal skills contribute to the team?

Answers to these questions will allow leaders to select best-fit employees who can hit the ground running and contribute to building the organization's future.

A surefire way of staying relevant was presented in this quote by Anthony J. D'Angelo: "Develop a passion for learning. If you do, you will never cease to grow."

When leaders continue to grow, they have the main ingredient for staying relevant themselves, and for keeping their organization relevant, and as a result, they not only add value but also increase their value to the organization.

In summary, a leader who stays relevant . . .

- Seeks feedback for self-improvement
- Regularly evaluates his or her professional competences
- Understands how he or she impacts the future of the organization
- Stays abreast of evolving demands and changes accordingly
- Looks ahead to his or her future and the future of the organization

SELF-REFLECTION
ADD VALUE

Now that you have more information about some of the behaviors and attributes associated with the Add Value principle, take a moment to reflect and rate yourself on your use of them.

INSTRUCTIONS

Read each statement below. **Use the 0–4 scale to rate yourself on how often you use the attribute described.**

0	1	2	3	4
NEVER	**RARELY**	**SOMETIMES**	**HALF THE TIME**	**MOST TIMES**

GOES BEYOND WHAT IS EXPECTED

		YOU
51	Consistently deliver more than what is expected or required	
52	Are perceived by others as an above-average performer	
53	Gain satisfaction from providing exceptional service to others	
54	Push the limits of what is expected	
55	Always see room for improvement	

SUBTOTAL SCORE

SHARES KNOWLEDGE & RESOURCES FREELY

		YOU ⬇
56	Unselfishly counsel team members on best approaches	
57	Document and share knowledge gained from past experiences	
58	Can be counted on to come through for others when needed	
59	Demonstrate knowledge and skills for others to learn	
60	Provide technical assistance to others	

SUBTOTAL SCORE ➔

EXHIBITS A PERSONAL LEADERSHIP BRAND

		YOU ⬇
61	Show consistency in your approach to leadership	
62	Are aware of your strengths, weaknesses, and emotions	
63	Are genuine in your interactions with others	
64	Are known for a particular style of leadership	
65	Demonstrate leadership traits that are unique to you	

SUBTOTAL SCORE ➔

DISPLAYS RESILIENCE

		YOU ⬇
66	Demonstrate a high level of stress-tolerance	
67	Hold yourself accountable for recovering from mistakes	
68	Maintain your physical and mental fitness	
69	Possess the ability to bounce back from past mistakes	
70	Demonstrate resolve to stay the course against adversity	

SUBTOTAL SCORE ➔

STAYS RELEVANT

		YOU
71	Seek feedback for self-improvement	
72	Regularly evaluate your professional competencies	
73	Understand how you impact the future of the organization	
74	Stay abreast of evolving demands and change accordingly	
75	Look ahead to your future and the future of the organization	

SUBTOTAL SCORE

± YOUR SCORE FOR THIS PRINCIPLE ±

	BEHAVIOR	SUBTOTAL SCORES
K	GOES BEYOND WHAT IS EXPECTED	
L	SHARES KNOWLEDGE & RESOURCES FREELY	
M	EXHIBITS A PERSONAL LEADERSHIP BRAND	
N	DISPLAYS RESILIENCE	
O	STAYS RELEVANT	

TOTAL SCORE

---

79 to 100 (High) — You demonstrate very effective use of this principle. Inspire and help others develop skills to successfully use it.

65 to 78 (Average) — You demonstrate effective use of this principle. Continue working to enhance your ability to use it.

Below 65 (Low) — You demonstrate limited use of this principle. Take advantage of opportunities to enhance your ability to use it.

For a more comprehensive evaluation, a companion 360° assessment (LEAD 360) is available with this book. The assessment allows members of your immediate work circle to assess the degree to which you exhibit the principles and behaviors discussed in this book.

Visit ***www.AlonzoJohnsonPHD.com*** *or* ***www.lead360assessment.com*** *for additional information on how to complete the LEAD 360 assessment.*

STAFF RELEVANT

17e	[illegible]	
18	[illegible]	
18a	[illegible]	
19	[illegible]	
19a	[illegible]	

SUBTOTAL SCORE: C

TOTAL SCORE FOR THIS PRINCIPLE

A	[illegible]	
B	[illegible]	
2a	[illegible] LEADERSHIP [illegible]	
B	[illegible]	
C	STAFF RELEVANT	

TOTAL SCORE: D

76 to 100 (High) — [illegible] use of this principle [illegible] and their effects [illegible]

45 to 75 (Average) — [illegible]

Below 45 (Low) — [illegible]

[illegible]

PRINCIPLE FOUR
DO THE RIGHT THING

For most of my childhood, I'd hear my parents use the phrase "do the right thing." And I have been admonished by others to do so throughout my professional career. I believe most of us want to do the right thing, but our desire to do so sometimes becomes convoluted with constraints like policies, procedures, and other external influences. For such a simple phrase, I found it challenging to fully comprehend at first. What is the right thing to do? And how will I know when to do it?

I have received many life lessons over the years that answered those questions. While serving a tour of duty with the US Army in South Korea, I had my first epiphany about doing the right thing.

It was on a cold January night (-50° F), on a tank gunnery range, that I heard the most profound statement I had ever heard about leadership. My battalion commander uttered the proclamation, "We are going to do this not because it's right, but because it's the right thing to do."

What the commander was referring to as "the right thing to do" was to have hot beverages (coffee, chocolate, and soup) available for the soldiers guarding the tanks and ammunition that night in subzero degree weather. While he wanted the soldiers to have as much as they needed to consume to stay warm, Army policy stipulated strict food service accountability.

I was impressed with the commander's position of "doing the right thing" as opposed to "doing things right." His statement resonated with me and set me on a path of doing the right things in my leadership endeavors.

Another "aha" experience about doing the right thing occurred in the private business sector. One of my responsibilities as a human resource (HR) leader was to assist other leaders who had employees with performance problems. One day a director, whom I had been advising on coaching an employee with a performance problem, stopped by my office to update me on the employee. He informed me that after almost a year of coaching, the employee's performance had not improved. And it seemed that the employee just wasn't working out. After much discussion, the director and I concluded that it was time to exit the employee from the organization.

I started the paperwork immediately and updated my boss, the senior vice president of HR, on our decision. After hearing about the employee's poor performance and the director's coaching efforts, my boss agreed that we should exit the employee from the organization, but with one caveat—we must wait until after the Christmas holidays.

We were about two weeks away from Christmas. He explained that exiting any employee during the Christmas holiday season was not the right thing to do.

Several years later, while taking a post graduate course, I discovered that both the battalion commander and senior VP of Human Resource's way of thinking was consistent with that of Warren Bennis, renowned researcher and author, who once said, "Managers are people who do things right and leaders are people who do the right thing."

The way Warren Bennis classified the manager and leader's roles was yet another epiphany for me. While the two are often used interchangeably, I came to realize that they are different. And although some managers lead and some leaders manage, the two activities are not synonymous.

Leaders who do the right thing seem to have something in common; they regularly demonstrate the following behaviors:

- ☐ **BALANCE LEADERSHIP AND MANAGEMENT**
- ☐ **DEMONSTRATE MORAL COURAGE**
- ☐ **ENCOURAGE OTHERS**
- ☐ **ASSESS THE SITUATION BEFORE ACTING**
- ☐ **COACH OTHERS**

BALANCING LEADERSHIP AND MANAGEMENT

Effectively manages day-to-day challenges while focusing on the vision for the future

---

The first behavior that we will discuss for the Doing the Right Thing principle is *balancing leadership and management.* Balance is of utmost importance, especially when it comes to leading and managing your team. How does a leader go about balancing the way he or she leads or manages when every team member is unique? How is leadership different from management, anyway?

One of the best places to look for help with that question is in the Army's Field Manual on leadership. According to the Manual, "leadership is influencing people—by providing purpose, direction, and motivation—while operating to accomplish the mission and improving the organization." The *American Heritage College Dictionary* defines management as "the person or persons who control or direct a business or other enterprise."

Leadership is focused on getting things done by influencing and motivating, and *management* is focused on getting things done by directing and controlling.

An effective leader must demonstrate the ability to use both leadership and management skills in a balanced way. Using too much of one as opposed to the other will likely negatively impact both the employees and organization.

There are naturally strong leaders and naturally strong managers. They often play to their strengths by frequently using skills and behaviors that are derived from their natural talents. This is not uncommon, since it is normal to do things that come natural to us. However, being strong in certain areas can result in overuse of our natural abilities, which can turn our strengths into weaknesses.

When anything is overused, there is a risk of achieving a negative impact. For example, if you use the same backhand swing all the time when playing tennis, you will likely overuse your elbow and develop tendonitis or bursitis. If you always use a confrontational style for handling conflict, you are not likely to be an effective leader. Leaders should strive to balance their strengths to achieve greater effectiveness.

However, with all the emphasis that has been placed on developing and using leadership skills recently, you may think that management skills are not important and should not be used. Truth is, the use of leadership and management skills is of equal importance; how and when they are executed will differentiate an effective leader from an ineffective leader.

Warren Bennis summed it up:

"Management is getting people to do what needs to be done. Leadership is getting people to want to do what needs to be done. Managers push. Leaders pull. Managers command. Leaders communicate."

Here is a side-by-side comparison of the leader and manager roles:

A LEADER...	A MANAGER...
Innovates for the future	Administers current resources
Strives for effectiveness	Strives for efficiency
Keeps eye on the horizon	Keeps eye on the bottom line
Asks "what" and "why"	Asks "how" and "when"
Is process-oriented	Is task-oriented
Empowers others	Controls others
Challenges status quo	Accepts status quo
Is concerned with overall direction	Is concerned with productivity
Focuses on the vision	Focuses on procedures
Asks thought-provoking questions	Provides answers

Managers perform five basic functions: planning, organizing, staffing, coordinating, and controlling. They operate in the present to maintain the status quo. Leaders, on the other hand, are **forward-thinking and have a clear view of what's necessary for future success.** They build teams by **inspiring and motivating others to share their vision.** And when there is a problem, they **seek to find solutions rather than someone to blame.** Leaders have the ability to identify trends and new ideas, and then motivate others to achieve them.

The difference between management and leadership is akin to the difference between the *transactional* and *transformational* styles of leadership. Let's explore each of them.

Transactional leaders (also referred to as *managerial leaders*) focus on the day-to-day running of the business rather than strategies for achieving the vision for the future. They maintain the status quo by ensuring that the routine work flows smoothly. Leaders who use this style **regularly schedule planning meetings with team members** to set goals and follow up on the progress of existing ones. They are usually authoritarians who get things done by

articulating clear performance goals and expectations to team members. And as the term *transactional* suggests, they accomplish goals by rewarding employees for performance.

Transformational leaders focus on the future to ensure the growth and success of their team members and the organization. They have a clear vision of success, and through proper planning, they execute strategically to achieve it. Transformational leaders are collaborators who get things done by setting goals and using intrinsic rewards and various forms of intrinsic motivation to encourage high levels of performance. They engage team members by identifying their higher-level needs, and then provide support to satisfy those needs. Additionally, transformational leaders build cohesive teams and provide personal and professional growth opportunities for each team member.

Both transactional and transformational styles of leadership are necessary for effective leadership. Some leaders start their careers being transactional, and then later evolve into becoming transformational. Bill Gates, founder and former CEO of Microsoft Corporation, is an example of a leader who has evolved over time.

Early in his career, Gates was very involved in overseeing the operations of Microsoft. His task-oriented autocratic (transactional) style of leadership was evident in his interactions with others with whom he worked—he was not comfortable with others having decision-making authority. He displayed uncanny intelligence and analytical skills, and he used this strength to hold staff accountable for achieving performance goals. He was results-driven, and used rewards (salaries and bonuses) as the primary means for achieving goals.

Over time, Gates' autocratic style of leadership could no longer keep pace with the expanding company. With more initiatives than he could personally oversee, he decided to hire the most talented employees he could find, and shift to a transformational style of leadership. This shift allowed him to delegate work, give team members more autonomy, and focus on the strategic aspect of Microsoft. He also adapted a participative style of leadership and motivated employees by providing growth opportunities and support.

Although Gates stepped down as Microsoft's CEO in 2000, he continued to offer transformational leadership as the Chairman of Microsoft and a philanthropist. In 2000, he, along with his wife, Melinda Gates, founded the largest private philanthropic foundation in the world. Its primary goals are to reduce poverty, enhance healthcare, and increase access to educational opportunities and information technology—to make lives better. This is the true mark of a transformational leader.

Although Gates' leadership style was more autocratic initially, he recognized the need to be a transformational leader to remain effective. Effective leaders are able to adapt their leadership styles according to the situation. For example, if a fire starts in the building, it would not be a great time to seek consensus on what to do. The leader is likely to be more successful using a transactional style of leadership to get everyone to safety. On the other hand, if a jetliner crashed in the wilderness, a transformational style of leadership will likely be more suitable for guiding the passengers to reach censuses on a survival strategy. Effective leaders use a balanced approach to leading and managing, because they recognize that balancing the two is necessary for success.

In summary, a leader who balances leadership and management . . .

- Articulates clear performance goals and expectations to team members
- Is forward-thinking with a clear view of what's necessary for future success
- Seeks to find solutions rather than someone to blame
- Regularly schedules planning meetings with team members
- Inspires and motivates others to share his or her vision

DEMONSTRATING MORAL COURAGE

Does the right thing even when it is not popular

Demonstrating moral courage is the next behavior that we will discuss for the Doing the Right Thing principle. The choice to do right or wrong is woven into the fabric of our everyday lives—we are constantly presented with opportunities to choose to do right, or wrong. It is admirable when someone chooses to do right. But, making the right choice and then floundering or demonstrating lack of conviction regarding that choice does not help the situation. When we choose to do right, we only show good moral reasoning, but when we act upon the choice to do right, and put ourselves at risk, in some way, we demonstrate moral courage.

To better understand what moral courage is, let's explore what is required in order for it to emerge. According to Rielle Miller, there are five requirements that must be present in order for moral courage to occur:

First, you must recognize that there is a moral issue to be resolved.

Second, you must choose how to deal with the moral issue. Your choice will usually be driven by personal values. Our personal values serve as the compass to our ethical beliefs and help us decide how to deal with moral issues.

Third, you must act upon the moral decision that you made earlier.

Fourth, you must take action(s) that put you at risk in some way and accept the consequences of your actions.

Fifth, you must face your fears and overcome them.

Leaders are frequently presented with ethical dilemmas; those who take action and do the right thing often do so because of their moral courage.

Malala Yousafzai, a Pakistani activist for women's education—and the youngest Nobel Prize recipient—is a great example of a leader who has demonstrated moral courage. After the Taliban took over her homeland in the Swat Valley region of Pakistan, they forbade girls from getting an education, banned them from attending school, and ordered all schools for girls closed.

Blogging under a pseudonym, and giving interviews for print and television media, Malala spoke out against the Taliban without regard to her personal safety. During her Nobel Prize acceptance speech, she recounted, "I had two options, one was to remain silent, and wait to be killed. And the second was to speak up, and then be killed. I chose the second one."

In Malala's case, all of the components of moral courage were present. She was confronted with the moral issue of the Taliban's mistreatment of women. She chose to deal with the issue and acted upon her choice by writing a blog and giving interviews to the media. She put herself at risk by taking action and overcame her fear of the Taliban's reprisal.

As a result of Malala speaking out against the injustices of the Taliban, an assassin shot her in the head in an attempt to silence her. The failed assassination attempt resulted in more scrutiny and resistance against the Taliban. It also sparked international support for Malala and her cause. She continues to speak out for women and children's rights throughout the world, and she has garnered global support for doing so.

Acts of moral courage are not only demonstrated in extreme situations, as in Malala's case. Each of us is presented with opportunities to exhibit it in our daily lives.

For example: a friend of mine, Susan, once worked in an office where some of the employees would place incoming paperwork for processing into their hold boxes and delay working on it until the weekend. Their goal was to create overflow work so that they could justify working during weekends to earn overtime pay. This practice seemed to increase when a major holiday was approaching, especially during the Christmas holiday season.

As the newest member assigned to the team, this struck Susan as unethical. She asked the employees participating in this practice to stop, but her request fell on deaf ears. Since she could not singlehandedly solve the problem at the source, her next action was to inform her boss, Todd. Todd was already aware of this overtime scheme and was allowing it to happen. So he did nothing to stop it.

Faced with the choice of "rocking the boat" or doing nothing to stop this overtime scheme, Susan decided on the former. She went straight to Todd's boss, David, and informed him about the matter. After learning of this scheme, David called Todd to his office to ask why so much overtime was required for such a small amount of work. When Todd could not answer the question to David's satisfaction, he was reprimanded for abusing overtime and informed that all future overtime work would require his approval.

Needless to say, Susan was not a popular person among those who had been abusing the overtime. She became known as "Miss Straight-Laced" within the team.

Earlier, I explored the importance of giving feedback as an extension of encouraging others. Some feedback requires moral courage from the leader. Some leaders cower at **giving honest feedback to team members about their work performance.** However, effective leaders are not afraid to give honest feedback; **they say what they mean and mean what they say.**

Another attribute of effective leaders is that they **do not postpone making tough or unpleasant decisions.** They have the moral courage to jump right in and **deal quickly and effectively with problems.** Since true leadership is **doing what is right despite the political climate or consequences,** moral courage is required for leadership effectiveness.

In summary, a leader who demonstrates moral courage . . .

- Does what is right despite the political climate or consequences
- Gives honest feedback to team members about their work performance
- Deals quickly and effectively with problems
- Does not postpone making tough or unpleasant decisions
- Says what he or she means and means what he or she says

ENCOURAGING OTHERS

Creates and maintains a supportive environment where people can grow

---

Encouraging others is another behavior displayed by leaders who do the right thing. Effective leaders know that acts of encouragement can inspire team members and influence the success of the organization; it is a behavior that provides great returns.

When leaders encourage employees, they build positive work relationships, maintain open communication, and build trust. A well-placed "thanks for coming through" or "I appreciate your extra effort" goes a long way towards helping employees feel appreciated, as well as creating a supportive work environment.

Employees working in supportive environments are usually more engaged; the high level of engagement results in increased productivity and a greater return (financial or otherwise) for the organization. These work environments also provide growth opportunities for employees by motivating them to accomplish more than they thought possible. John Maxwell said, "People go farther than they thought they could when someone else thinks they can."

Sports teams provide great examples of encouragement in action. At almost any sporting event, you are likely to see team members "high fiving" and encouraging each other to keep up the pace. They often push each other to succeed and win, even when the scores are not in their favor.

Whether in sports or business environment, encouraging others seems to build positive relationships and increase productivity. But what approach should leaders use to encourage others?

Leaders who encourage others possess a variety of attributes. Research shows that the following attributes are among the most salient for encouraging others:

- **Being patient**
- **Giving feedback**
- **Providing guidance and support**
- **Being a good listener**
- **Giving recognition**

Let's take a closer look at how each of these attributes can serve as a beneficial tool for encouraging others.

We have all heard the expression that "**patience** is a virtue." And most of us need the virtue of patience to be effective leaders. This is especially true when a team member is learning a new task; it often takes time to perfect new learning. Being patient as he or she acquires the skills and knowledge required for the new task will make the learning experience less stressful for everyone involved. And in the high-paced, get-it-done-now environments of today's work world, empathy is the key to patience. Putting yourself in the employee's shoes will often remind you of the challenges that you experienced when you were learning a new task; empathy allows you to see things from the employee's perspective and build more patience.

Giving feedback is a useful tool for encouraging others. In fact, Kenneth Blanchard, author, speaker, and business management consultant, says that "feedback is the breakfast of champions." And since breakfast is arguably the most important meal of the day, feedback provides energy for growth and development.

From youth throughout adulthood, humans crave positive feedback and usually respond well to it. As a child, most of us received more than our fair share of positive feedback to reinforce learning new skills or meeting a milestone (such as walking, feeding ourselves, and personal hygiene). But once we grew up and entered the workplace, the feedback likely diminished, unless we did something wrong. However, feedback should be an ongoing process, not just when something goes wrong.

Feedback is most effective when it is specific and balanced. For example, "you haven't been paying attention to your work lately," is not as specific as "you had too many errors in your monthly report." And when you are providing the employee with constructive feedback, balance it with a positive contribution that he or she has made.

Guidance and support encourage team members and create the right conditions for them to thrive. According to Maslow's Hierarchy of Needs theory, people are motivated to seek self-actualization, given the right conditions. Effective leaders know how to tap into this motivation by providing employees with guidance and support to create growth opportunities.

Effective leaders genuinely care about those whom they lead and have their best interest at heart. Leaders show their team members that they care in many ways. Here are a few examples:

- Discuss their future with them to help identify options for achieving their career goals.
- Give them assignments that are challenging but manageable (stretch assignments) to help develop skills and knowledge consistent with their goals.
- Allow them to share their talents with the rest of the organization to gain exposure.
- Introduce them to others who have experience in areas that are consistent with their goals.
- Provide team members shadowing experiences, attending meetings that are of interest to them, when appropriate.
- Coach or mentor them.

Listening to someone, in and of itself, is an act of encouragement. Oftentimes employees don't want you to tell them what to do, they just need an ear to listen to their ideas and help them think things through. When those occasions arise, be there for them and listen actively by keeping the following guidelines in mind:

- Listen to their perspective.
- Resist the urge to talk while they are talking.
- Show interest and encourage them to speak.
- Summarize the discussion periodically.
- Ask questions that rephrase or recap their own comments to confirm understanding, show empathy, and encourage them to elaborate. For example: "So you believe you could have achieved this goal if you had more time?"

Being appreciated is a fundamental human desire. So it is not surprising that in the business world, appreciation ranks high on the list of acts that motivate employees. Leaders who show appreciation to their team members by recognizing them are validating that their contributions are valued, and they are a significant part of the team.

Employee **recognition** can be formal, or informal, and is easy to do; however, recognizing team members should be planned and done right. An unplanned recognition may be perceived as disingenuous. The four steps below outline a simple process for recognizing others:

1. Thank the person being recognized in person and by name.
2. State what he or she did specifically to warrant recognition. Be sure to include specifics, because it helps to reinforce that behavior.
3. Explain what value his or her accomplishment added to the team and the organization.
4. Conclude by thanking him or her again by name, and describe the emotion that you feel (pride, gratitude, respect, etc.) because of his or her accomplishment.

Here is an example of using the four steps to give recognition.

"Jon, thank you for coming in last weekend to finish the survey analyses and the proposal for the employee engagement project. Your efforts allowed our team to submit three additional proposals to our clients this quarter and put us ahead of our target. I realize that you sacrificed your weekend to do this, and I appreciate your efforts very much, Jon! Let's discuss some time off to compensate for coming in last weekend."

Remember, everyone wants to be appreciated, and showing appreciation through recognition fulfills this desire. Effective leaders are quick to recognize others as a way of acknowledging their contributions and motivating them to continue adding value as team members.

In summary, a leader who encourages others . . .

- Is patient with team members when they are learning a new skill
- Provides constant on-the-spot feedback to team members
- Gives employees guidance and support concerning career progression
- Is a good listener when others just want to talk things out
- Takes the time to recognize others for their contributions and achievements

---

ASSESSING THE SITUATION BEFORE ACTING

Evaluates the situation and selects the best course of action before plunging in

---

The third behavior that we will discuss for the Doing the Right Thing principle is *assessing the situation before acting.* The old adage "look before you leap" suggests that one should evaluate the situation before plunging in. It is not prudent to act without first considering the possible consequences. Yet, many leaders are prone to jumping right in and taking charge of initiatives without having all the facts.

Effective leaders don't plunge into situations hastily. They give forethought to possible outcomes. They **examine multiple explanations and consider all relevant data when solving problems** and **rarely make decisions before hearing all the facts.** The consequences of not doing so may result in conclusions and decisions that are not fact-based—in other words, poor decisions. Poor decisions can result in the loss of your credibility; the perception that you are a "loose cannon"; they can even rob you of the trust that others have in you and damage your leadership brand. No organization is immune to poor decisions caused by jumping to conclusions. It happens in large and small organizations, from local to enterprise levels. Considering all available facts first will position you to make the most prudent decisions possible.

An example of an idea that was not objectively borne out by all the facts can be seen in the launch of New Coke in 1985. New Coke was launched to replace the original formula, which had not been changed for 99 years. However, with Pepsi-Cola soft drink capturing more shares of the cola market, the Coca-Cola Company's leaders were under incessant pressure to regain market shares. They concluded that changing the taste of the original flagship Coke would position them to compete with the sweeter-tasting Pepsi.

Market research using taste testing focus groups, and surveys for New Coke, found that about 10 to 12% of the focus group participants were not happy with the new product replacing the original formula. Some focus group members even stated that they might stop drinking Coke altogether if the original Coke were replaced. But since the survey data indicated that the new formula was viewed more favorably, Coke's leaders made the decision to launch New Coke to replace their flagship brand, without considering customers' passion and emotional attachment to the brand—as echoed by some of the focus group members. Within a week of launching New Coke, production of the original Coke stopped.

To say the least, New Coke was not embraced as expected, especially in the Southeastern part of the US. In fact, a large percentage of US-based customers boycotted the new product. It caused such a backlash that Coke's leaders decided to re-launch the original brand (now labeled Coke Classic) fewer than three months after New Coke hit the market.

In this example, it appeared Coke did everything right as far as market analysis was concerned. So why did this venture fail? The level of objectivity during the analysis phase was breached. We humans have a tendency to see what we want to see when analyzing data. In their haste to reclaim cola market shares, The Coca-Cola Company's leaders did not properly weigh the fact that dissenting focus group members were a representative sample of the general population. And if they rejected the new product, a large segment of the population would likely reject it as well.

When analyzing data upon which decisions will be based, it is important to remain objective and **assess all options before selecting the most viable one to solve the problem.** Despite conducting numerous taste tests on New Coke, leaders failed to adequately assess consumers' perceptions of the original brand.

When questioning the dissenting focus group members, Coke's leaders failed to ask *"**why**" questions more than "**what**" questions.* Asking *why* is key to assessing any situation. The 5 Whys problem solving technique is a simple, yet powerful tool that can be used to find the root cause of almost any problem. Each time "Why" is asked and answered, the underlying problem becomes more evident. Using this technique correctly, in the case of New Coke, might have brought out the real reason that was behind their declining market shares and would have prevented The Coca-Cola Company's leadership from launching another product. Here is an example of how the technique could have been used to determine the root cause of the dissent from focus group members:

Some focus groups members don't want New Coke. (Problem)
Why? Customers are motivated by more than taste. (Why #1)
Why? Customers enjoy the familiarity of the original Coke. (Why #2)
Why? Customers are passionate about the original Coke. (Why #3)
Why? Customers are emotionally attached to the original Coke. (Why #4)
Why? Customers view the original Coke as a symbol of significance. (Why #5 and Root Cause)

Effective leaders not only ask *why* questions a lot, but they also do not cherry pick the data. Cherry picking what data gets analyzed is as bad as not doing an analysis at all. Pressure to compete with Pepsi may have caused Coke's leaders to cherry pick the data that favored their inclination.

Although effective leaders **draw on experience and available resources to guide decisions and actions,** in the Coca-Cola example, changing the formula of Coke's flagship product had not been done before. So there wasn't any experience available to inform the challenge at hand. Even so, better use of the focus group's data, which was an available resource, might have prevented this significant mishap. Analyzing data from multiple sources, even sources that might not have seemed significant, would have allowed Coke's leaders to **assess all options, and then select the most viable one to solve the problem.**

In summary, a leader who assesses the situation before acting . . .

- Rarely makes decisions until he or she has heard all the facts
- Examines multiple explanations and considers all relevant data when solving problems
- Asks "why questions" more than "what questions"
- Assesses all options then selects the most viable one to solve a problem
- Draws on experience and available resources to guide actions and decisions

---

COACHING OTHERS

Guides others in decision-making and/or developing skills and abilities to improve their performance

---

The last behavior that we will explore for the Doing the Right Thing principle is *coaching others.* Building leadership capacity or bench strength for the future success of the organization is one of the most important tasks that leaders perform. Coaching is arguably the most effective tool to help leaders accomplish that task.

Leaders use coaching for a myriad of reasons. From **helping others assess their skills and determining how to broaden them**, to **helping them recognize and eliminate unproductive behavior**, coaching is an indispensable tool for developing others.

Coaching is not telling others what to do; rather, it is **encouraging others to find their own solutions to problems.** Coaches employ a variety of skills, such as probing questioning techniques and interpersonal communication. Effective coaches **are perceived as good sounding boards**, and they **listen attentively to others to help guide their decision-making.** As a leader, it is your responsibility to maintain proficient coaching skills and be familiar with and use all available tools to help develop others.

The GROW Model is a tool that has been used to coach and develop others. It was developed in the 1980s by Allen Fine, Graham Alexander, and Sir John Whitmore. It is one of the most widely used coaching models available to help individuals clarify what they want to accomplish and determine how to accomplish it. This four-step model consists of the following components:

1. Setting **G**oals
2. Examining Current **R**eality
3. Considering **O**ptions
4. Determining the **W**ay Forward

SETTING GOALS

The first step in the GROW Model is *setting goals*. Goals are used in this instance to help the individual you are coaching determine what he or she wants to achieve. These goals may also be described as objectives, targets, key results, or outcome achievements. Regardless of what they are called, the question to be answered during this step of the model is "What is the individual's aim or desired result?"

As we discussed earlier, when setting goals, use the acronym SMART:

Specific—It is clear, unambiguous, and answers the "what," "why," "who," "where," and "which" questions.
Measurable—It presents measurable criteria and answers the "how much," "how many," and "how will I know when it is accomplished" questions.
Attainable—It is achievable within the environment using given resources.
Relevant—It is appropriate for the situation and consistent with other initiatives.
Timely—It can be completed within an appropriate time-frame.

Using the SMART acronym as a guide is essential for developing actionable and definable goals.

EXAMINING CURRENT REALITY

The next step in the GROW Model is *examining the current reality*. If the goal clarifies what the employee you are coaching is to accomplish, then an examination of the current reality lets him or her know where to start. It also allows the individual to identify the work that has to be done to close the gap between the current state and what needs to be accomplished.

When identifying current realities, one should avoid false assumptions. Obtaining feedback from others helps to check for false assumptions.

It is important to develop a detailed understanding of the current reality. Consider the tools available, skills, knowledge, networks, and support in order to identify potential resources that may be useful.

Questions to ask when examining current reality include the following:

- Will the current environment support your efforts?
- Do you have the required skills and knowledge, or will you have to acquire them?
- How can you leverage your network to support this initiative?
- Whom will you have to involve?
- Do you have the necessary support system and budget, if required?
- What obstacles do you anticipate encountering?

Answers to these questions will help bring the current reality into clearer focus.

CONSIDERING OPTIONS

After you determine what the person you are coaching wants to accomplish (goals) and identify his or her starting point (reality), the other step in the GROW Model is to generate some possible ways that he or she can accomplish these goals. Start by generating options that are strategic-level, and then move to the tactical and operational-level details for planning purposes. The most important thing to remember during this step is to identify as many options as possible and not to look for the "one right way." Be innovative and brainstorm to identify multiple viable options.

When choosing the final option to pursue, consider the cost-benefit and risk of each option. The second or third options that were not selected may serve as contingency options, if the first option does not work out as expected. Some useful questions that should be asked when considering options include the following:

- Has a full range of options been identified?
- How will the final option be selected?
- What are the cost-benefits and risks of each option?
- What resources are required for each option?
- Which option represents the best approach?
- Which options should serve as contingencies?

Once this step is complete, the person you are coaching should have a plan to accomplish his or her goals, or at the least, a solid framework for a plan.

DETERMINING THE WAY FORWARD

It's now time to make the plan or framework you developed actionable. The final step of the GROW Model is determining the way forward. In other words, the person you are coaching will need to make his or her actions specific and identify timing to maximize the achievement of his or her goals.

Another consideration during this step is whether everyone involved in helping the person you are coaching has the motivation for the journey.

Questions that can help include the following:

- What are the specific steps and timing for each action?
- Do you have the required support and resources?
- What obstacles do you anticipate encountering?
- Do you have the motivation to tackle this initiative?
- How can you sustain this goal, once achieved?

In summary, a leader who coaches others . . .

- Helps others assess their skills and determine how to broaden them
- Helps others recognize and eliminate unproductive behavior
- Listens attentively to others to help guide their decision making process
- Is perceived by others as a good sounding board
- Encourages team members to find their own solutions to problems

SELF-REFLECTION

DO THE RIGHT THING

Now that you have more information about some of the behaviors and attributes associated with the Do the Right Thing principle, take a moment to reflect and rate yourself on your use of them.

INSTRUCTIONS

Read each statement below. **Use the 0–4 scale to rate yourself on how often you use the attribute described.**

0	1	2	3	4
NEVER	**RARELY**	**SOMETIMES**	**HALF THE TIME**	**MOST TIMES**

BALANCES LEADERSHIP & MANAGEMENT

		YOU
76	Articulate clear performance goals and expectations to team members	
77	Forward-thinking and have a clear view of what's necessary for success	
78	Seek to find solutions rather than someone to blame	
79	Regularly schedule planning meetings with team members	
80	Inspire and motivate others to share your vision	

SUBTOTAL SCORE

DEMONSTRATES MORAL COURAGE

		YOU
81	Do what is right despite the political climate or consequences	
82	Give honest feedback to team members about their work performance	
83	Deal quickly and effectively with problems	
84	Don't postpone making tough or unpleasant decisions	
85	Say what you mean and mean what you say	

SUBTOTAL SCORE

ENCOURAGES OTHERS

		YOU
86	Patient with team members when they are learning a new skill	
87	Provide constant on-the-spot feedback to team members	
88	Give employees guidance and support concerning career progression	
89	Are a good listener when others just want to talk things out	
90	Take the time to recognize others for their contributions/achievements	

SUBTOTAL SCORE

ASSESSES THE SITUATION BEFORE ACTION

		YOU
91	Rarely make decisions until hearing all the facts	
92	Examine multiple explanations and consider all relevant data	
93	Ask "why" questions more than "what" questions	
94	Assess all options, then select the most viable one to solve problems	
95	Draw on experience and available resources to guide actions/decisions	

SUBTOTAL SCORE

COACHES OTHERS

		YOU ➊
96	Help others assess their skills and determine how to broaden them	
97	Help others recognize and eliminate unproductive behavior	
98	Listen attentively to others to help guide their decision-making process	
99	Are perceived by others as a good sounding board	
100	Encourage team members to find their own solutions to problems	

SUBTOTAL SCORE ➋

± YOUR SCORE FOR THIS PRINCIPLE ±

	BEHAVIOR	SUBTOTAL SCORES
P	BALANCES LEADERSHIP & MANAGEMENT	
Q	DEMONSTRATES MORAL COURAGE	
R	ENCOURAGES OTHERS	
S	ASSESSES THE SITUATION BEFORE ACTION	
T	COACHES OTHERS	

TOTAL SCORE ➋

---

79 to 100 (High) — You demonstrate very effective use of this principle. Inspire and help others develop skills to successfully use it.

65 to 78 (Average) — You demonstrate effective use of this principle. Continue working to enhance your ability to use it.

Below 65 (Low) — You demonstrate limited use of this principle. Take advantage of opportunities to enhance your ability to use it.

For a more comprehensive evaluation, a companion 360° assessment (LEAD 360) is available with this book. The assessment allows members of your immediate work circle to assess the degree to which you exhibit the principles and behaviors discussed in this book.

*Visit **www.AlonzoJohnsonPHD.com** or **www.lead360assessment.com** for additional information on how to complete the LEAD 360 assessment.*

CONCLUSION

Leading Made Easy presents a straightforward approach to leadership effectiveness. Using the acronym LEAD to present four principles (**L**earn from Mistakes, **E**xemplify Competence, **A**dd Value, and **D**o the Right Thing) makes this leadership concept easy to remember and employ. Each principle has five associated behaviors that are building blocks to guide your effectiveness as a leader. The principles originate from tried-and-true concepts that make leading easy by enabling you to avoid or overcome stumbling blocks that you will encounter along your leadership journey.

Many leaders have used the LEAD principles in different environments and leadership roles and have found them to be essential elements for effectiveness and success.

Such was the case with Jon Alson, a director for a Fortune 500 company. One day his boss phoned him to ask if he would consider relocating to corporate headquarters for a temporary but challenging new role within the HR department. Jon's company had just negotiated a multi-billion-dollar deal to acquire part of another company, along with some of its brands. Jon's boss needed someone to lead the HR team to restructure and integrate new staff into the expanded organization. Viewing this as a stretch assignment with growth opportunities, Jon accepted it, relocated to the corporate headquarters, and immediately began putting together an integration team.

While leading the integration team, he used the LEAD principles to create a leadership framework to guide his actions. The principles served as a multiplier, allowing Jon and his small eleven-person team to integrate over 2,000 employees on two continents into the organization in only five months after the deal closed. Leading an integration that resulted in doubling the size of Jon's organization and increasing its global footprint was quite an accomplishment, since this was the first major acquisition for the company, and there were no policies or rulebooks for Jon to follow.

Jon remembers how beneficial it was to leverage the LEAD principles and their underlying behaviors during this assignment.

Of course, Jon made a few errors along the way, but he greatly benefited from them as he **learned from his mistakes.** He recalls that merely accepting the assignment labeled him as a *risk taker.* And since he had not served in such a role before, he also had to be *open to new ideas*, and *accept mistakes as opportunities.* Jon acquired much of the knowledge that was required for his team's success by *learning on the fly*. To be effective and remain relevant in his role, Jon had to stay abreast of international labor laws, create the right retention strategies for critical employees, transfer knowledge across continents, and integrate incompatible human resources information systems.

While quickly learning new job requirements, Jon still managed to **exemplify competence** by *exhibiting a wealth of skills* and *acting as a source of knowledge* in other areas. Overseeing the redesign of the organization and helping employees transition from a legacy culture to a new one are two examples of how Jon demonstrated these two attributes. Jon *displayed expert power* in his role as team leader and *set the example* for team members and the employees from the acquired company. This was an important factor for *building trust* and allaying the fears of the acquired employees as they merged into their new company.

As Jon continues to reflect on his integration experience, he recounts the many ways in which he **added value** in this role. He developed integration guidelines to ensure consistency across continents, while onboarding the new employees. He also *shared his knowledge and resources freely* to ensure a successful merger and set the stage for change. This role required long hours and extensive travel. It seemed that Jon was always on an airplane—sometimes traveling to as many as three countries (England, Spain, and

Germany) in as many days. He not only fulfilled the demands of the job but also *displayed resilience* and *went beyond what was expected.* Jon *exhibited a personal leadership brand* throughout the integration process that was unique to him—his boss branded him as a visionary who leads from the front.

Jon's quest to **do the right thing** in this role was evident by his willingness to *balance leadership and management* of the team. He skillfully oversaw the day-to-day running of the team (training team members, assigning tasks, and meeting milestones), while focusing on the future of the organization. This was by far the toughest job that Jon had ever done. One reason was that Jon's team members lacked experience—no one on the team had worked on an integration project before. Undaunted, Jon ensured that each team member was trained in his or her area of responsibility, then *coached* and *encouraged* them to ensure their success and the success of the organization.

There were decisions that Jon had to make about employees during the integration period that summoned his *moral courage* and forethought to *assess the situation before acting.*

If Jon's story has a ring of familiarity, you have probably led (or been) a member of a special project team in the past. It is certainly familiar to me because I was Jon (or Jon was me) during my tenure in the corporate business world. Jon's story is one of many examples of how I have used and authenticated the LEAD principles through research and years of leadership experience in the military, education, and private business sector.

I can attest to the utility of these principles. It is my hope that using them will not only enhance your ability to lead effectively, but also make your job as a leader **easy.**

SUGGESTED READINGS

Bennis, Warren. *Managing People is Like Herding Cats: Warren Bennis on Leadership.* Executive Excellence Publishing, 1999.

Blank, Warren. *The 108 Skills of Natural Born Leaders.* AMACOM, 2001.

Brooks, Robert and Sam Goldstein. *The Power of Resilience. Achieving Balance, Confidence, and Personal Strength in Your Life.* McGraw-Hill Education, 2004.

Carson, Clayborne. *The Papers of Martin Luther King, Jr: Threshold of a New Decade, January 1959–December 1960.* University of California Press, 2005.

Collins, Jim. *Good to Great: Why Some Companies Make the Leap . . . And Others Don't.* HarperBusiness, 2001.

Conley, Chip. *Peak: How Great Companies Get Their Mojo from Maslow.* Jossey-Bass, 2007.

Covey, Stephen. *The Speed of Trust: The One Thing That Changes Everything.* Free Press; Reprint edition, 2006.

George, Bill and David Gergen. *Discover Your True North. Becoming an Authentic Leader.* Jossey-Bass, 2015.

Goldsmith, Marshall and Mark Reiter. *Triggers: Creating Behavior That Lasts—Becoming the Person You Want to Be.* Crown Business, 2015.

Greenleaf, Robert K. *The Servant as Leader.* The Greenleaf Center for Servant Leadership, 2015.

Johnson, Alonzo. *Hiring Made Easy as PIE: The Hiring Manager's Guide to Selecting the Best-Fit Employee.* OASYS Press, 2015.

Landsberg, Max. *The Tao of Coaching: Boost Your Effectiveness at Work by Inspiring and Developing Those Around You.* Profile Books, 2015.

Maxwell, John. *Failing Forward: Turning Mistakes into Stepping Stones for Success.* Thomas Nelson; Reprint edition, 2007.

Schultz, Duane P. and Sydney Ellen Schultz. *Theories of Personality*; 10th edition. Cengage Learning, 2012.

Sinek, Simon. *Leaders Eat Last: Why Some Teams Pull Together and Others Don't.* Portfolio, 2014.

Terry, Robert W. *Authentic Leadership: Courage in Action.* Jossey-Bass, 1993.

Thompson, Henry L. *The Stress Effect: Why smart leaders do dumb things, and what to do about it.* Jossey-Bass, 2010.

Treasurer, Bill. *Leaders Open Doors, 2nd Edition: A Radically Simple Leadership Approach to Lift People, Profits, and Performance.* Association for Talent Development, 2015.

Whitmore, John. *Coaching for Performance: GROWing Human Potential and Purpose - The Principles and Practice of Coaching and Leadership*, 4th Edition. Nicholas Brealey, 2009.

Zoeller, Hope and Joe DeSensi. *HOPE for Leaders Unabridged.* Red Letter Publishing, 2015.

ABOUT THE AUTHOR

Alonzo Johnson, Ph.D., is the Managing Partner of The OASYS Group, a talent management consulting company. He has held leadership positions in the military, higher education, and in the private business sector. Alonzo has over three decades of experience in talent management and human resources. His expertise includes staffing, organizational, and people development.

He specializes in creating and conducting leadership programs for a global audience and implementing a variety of talent assessment processes. He is the developer of the LEAD 360° assessments and other value-added leadership assessment tools, and is certified to administer and interpret the results of various psychometrics (Emotional Quotient Inventory 2.0®, Emotional Quotient 360®, FIRO Element B™, Judgment Index™, Myers-Briggs Type Indicator®, etc.).

ABOUT THE OASYS GROUP

The OASYS Group is a management consulting company. The mission of the company is to *help people grow* by providing talent management solutions for every stage of employment—from recruiting and onboarding new employees to engaging, developing, and retaining existing employees. The OASYS Group's core strategy is to align performance management processes with business goals. The competency-based approach creates a synchronized work environment in which employees are engaged, thereby increasing performance and reducing turnover.

The OASYS Group's consultants are passionate about leadership development. They take an unusual, but systematic approach to developing leaders by leveraging three critical factors: assessment, assignment and association. These critical factors are articulated as the AAA model. First, assessments are administered to the leader and the results are used to identify opportunities for growth. Next, work assignments that will provide stretch-goals are explored and identified. This assignment can be leading a project team within the leader's current role, or serving in a different role altogether--as long as the assignment affords growth opportunities. Finally, leaders develop associations that provide coaching or mentoring in the areas identified for improvement.

Sometimes leaders require more individualized help to achieve their goals. The OASYS Group employs a variety of coaching tools and strategies to help leaders realize their goals.

www.ingramcontent.com/pod-product-compliance
Lightning Source LLC
Chambersburg PA
CBHW021107210326
41598CB00016B/1368

* 9 7 8 0 9 8 6 3 9 6 5 3 3 *